Twayne's United States Authors Series

Kenneth Patchen

TUSAS 292

Courtesy of Arthur Knight

Kenneth Patchen (1957)

KENNETH PATCHEN

By LARRY R. SMITH

Bowling Green State University
Firelands Campus

TWAYNE PUBLISHERS
A DIVISION OF G. K. HALL & CO., BOSTON

Library of Congress Cataloging in Publication Data

Smith, Larry R
    Kenneth Patchen.

    (Twayne's United States authors series ; TUSAS 292)
    Bibliography: p. 183-90
    Includes index.
    1.   Patchen, Kenneth, 1911-1972—Criticism and
interpretation.
PS3531.A764Z88   811'.5'4   77-13758
ISBN 0-8057-7195-6

Contents

About the Author

Larry R. Smith received his B.A. from Muskingum College (1965); his M.A. (1969) and Ph.D. (1974) from Kent State University. Dr. Smith is an Assistant Professor of English at Bowling Green State University's Firelands Campus in Huron, Ohio, where he has taught since 1970. Prior to that, he taught at Euclid Senior High School in Euclid, Ohio, 1965-1968. At Firelands Campus Dr. Smith teaches courses in film, world literature, creative writing, and the Modern and Contemporary Periods of Literature. For the past five years he has conducted the Firelands Experimental Film Festival for northwestern Ohio.

Professor Smith has published film and literary criticism and does book reviews for the Toledo *Blade*. In 1976 Dr. Smith collected his poetry, which had been published in a variety of literary magazines, into the book *Growth: Poems and Sketches* (Bigfork, Minnesota: Northwoods Press, 1976). He has done readings from his poetry and prose at high schools and colleges, and is currently at work on a collection of surrealist writings. His work has appeared in the following "Little" magazines: *Best of Poetry 1973, Cardinal Poetry Quarterly, Expressive Arts Review, Firelands Fine Arts Review I, II, III, From the Hills, Ghost Dance, The Mixer, Notable American Poets, Poetry Now.* His current research interests are: literature of place, American Surrealism, the San Francisco Renaissance, and the work of Paul Blackburn and James Tate. The author received a National Endowment for the Humanities grant to study Surrealism at Syracuse University in 1976, and he was a Poetry Contributor at the 1977 Breadloaf Writers' Conference in Vermont.

Preface

Kenneth Patchen combines a hard realism with a visionary idealism. Writing of societal madness yet of man's capacity for love and
beauty, Patchen remains a forgotten conscience to mankind — his
art a vivid reminder of all the evil and good that we are. Defying
objective analysis of reader and critic, he creates an art marked by
its social and moral relevance, its prolific output, its radical experi-
mentalism, and its extreme individuality. Using art as his tool, he
aspired to perform the function of poet-prophet for mankind, leading man from darkness to light. Such is the universal and worldly
character of Patchen's art.

Present critical attempts to categorize his art have resulted in distortion and neglect. This study will overcome these weaknesses by
addressing itself to Patchen's extreme independence both as an
artist and as a man — a concept which is crucial for understanding
the form and function of his work. Maintaining the critical objec-
tivity possible while remaining receptive to Patchen's apocalyptic
vision, I would hope to make his art more truly 'available.' In an
attempt to present a clear overview of his basic vision and impres-
sive achievement, detailed analysis of his major works beyond *The
Journal of Albion Moonlight* is only approximated here. Although
it would be tempting after Patchen's death in 1972 to attempt a
"summing up," the real intent is for an "opening up" of the relevant and daring experimental art of this American writer.

Approaching Patchen as an individual artist then requires some
understanding of his life, and because the facts of his life are not
generally well known, the first chapter attempts to compile the scattered biographical details. I thank Miriam Patchen for her generous
assistance in establishing a chronology. Though Patchen was never
a regionalist nor a confessionalist, his life experiences, comprised
of equal shares of pain and beauty, play a crucial role in shaping his
vision of existence. Patchen's biography reveals a molding of
character, a shaping of the proletarian youth of a Midwestern
American steel town into the activist and avant-garde artist of

Greenwich Village and later of San Francisco. From his active childhood in Niles and Warren, Ohio, to his final bedridden years in Palo Alto, California, Patchen remained a sensitive and compassionate artist. As he believed that the artist must be one with his life, that his life is his greatest work of art, Patchen's adjustment to the physical and mental torture which he endured helped to form his life and art. The first chapter attempts to demonstrate sources and resolutions for Patchen's seemingly paradoxical vision — where the madness of man's violence, corruption, and waste are united with his perception of the beauty and wonder of life, of the capacity for achieving love between a man and a woman, and ultimately of a compassionate commitment to all of life.

Given an overview of Patchen's tripartite life vision of "man's madness," a necessary "engagement," an ideal "wonder," the overall shape of his work can be suggested. The second chapter relates this vision of life to his vision of art through the role of poet-prophet, which he adopted from William Blake. Patchen's own functional aesthetics are revealed, in particular, in his long poem on the artist's duty from *The Journal of Albion Moonlight*.

The third, fourth and fifth chapters attempt to define and demonstrate Patchen's basic three part vision of life and art. "An Art of Madness" reveals his essential witness to the societal insanities of violence, capitalist corruptions, and an accepted conditioning to the absurdities of man. His art is disclosed as dedicated to curing this sickness through an open recognition and a consequent rejection of "man's madness." In "An Art of Engagement" Patchen's art is shown to be committed to the goals of love, brotherhood, a unity of life, and the necessity for engaged belief. The results are the aesthetic-social goals of "personalism" of style, and the joint ideals of the "total book" and the "total artist." "An Art of Wonder" demonstrates the Romantic basis for Patchen's state of "wonder" as based on a belief in the ideal life approach as one of freedom, imagination, spontaneous innocence, and an openness to the universe. His art is shown to be dedicated to creating in and presenting models of "wonder."

With these basic principles of Patchen's associated view of life and art, we can proceed to a close examination of the art produced. Because virtually all of Patchen's art is radically experimental, it will be presented according to the experimental forms which he created. In the sixth chapter, following a review of all the experimental prose, Patchen's masterpiece, his anti-novel *The Journal of Albion Moonlight*, is analyzed in detail. Patchen's progressive merger of poetry and prose modes is shown in the seventh chapter as developing from the crude juxtapositions of *First Will and Testament*, to the simultaneous printed texts of *The Journal of Albion Moonlight* and *Sleeper's Awake*, to the gradual blending of "poems-in-prose" found in *Panels for the Walls of Heaven*, and culminating in the contemporary synthesis of the prose poem found in *The Famous Boating Party* and *Poemscapes*.

The eighth chapter reveals Patchen as a pioneer innovator in the concrete poetry form. Comparing Patchen's concrete art in *Sleepers Awake*, *Panels*, and *Cloth of the Tempest* with the aesthetics of the Concrete Poetry Movement is mutually revealing. The ninth chapter presents Patchen as a founder and main force in the Poetry-and-Jazz Movement in America's late 1950's. Together with Kenneth Rexroth and Lawrence Ferlinghetti, Patchen fostered the movement and made its highest achievement in developing his "poetry-jazz" form. A chronicling of the period as well as a close analysis of Patchen's contribution is presented.

Writing in what may be termed his "wonder period" — from middle 1950's to his death in 1972 — Patchen's concern for social reform turned increasingly to one of personal growth through "wonder" as man's last hope for societal salvation. The tenth chapter examines his unique form of irrational tales and verse, developed first in *Fables and Other Little Tales* and followed by *Hurrah for Anything* and *Because It Is* — Patchen's poetry of the absurd. The growing merger of painting and writing forms is presented in the eleventh chapter. His initial development of "painted books," with individually author painted covers, progressed to a merger of "poems and drawings," the juxtaposition of a drawing with an irrational tale or verse, and culminated in the total synthesis of Patchen's unique "picture-poem" form in *But Even So, Hallelujah Anyway,* and *Wonderings*. While these graphics can only be discussed here, a close examination of them openly reveals Patchen's vision.

The final chapter suggests some conclusions concerning the reassessment of Patchen's place in American and world literature. His emergence as a model of the contemporary artist of involvement follows increased attention by scholarly critics of radically experimental work. In particular, the needed bibliography is offered as a starting point for future scholarly study.

Acknowledgments

I wish to express my appreciation for the initial advice and encouragement of Glenn S. Burne, Jonathan Williams, Frederick Eckman, and James Russell Lowell. I am also grateful for the valuable suggestions of Professors Wayne E. Kvam, Bernard Benstock, and especially Sanford E. Marovitz. I was generously assisted by Dean Keller and the Special Collections Division of Kent State University Library, which houses significant Patchen material.

To Mrs. Miriam Patchen I owe particular thanks for her cooperation, advice, materials, and her kindness. And to my wife Ann and my family I owe thanks for constant encouragement and understanding.

I wish to express my gratitude to New Directions Publishing Corporation for permission to quote from and to reproduce copyrighted material from:

Acknowledgments

Kenneth Patchen, *Hallelujah Anyway*. Copyright © 1966 by Kenneth Patchen.

Kenneth Patchen, *Wonderings*. Copyright © 1971 by Kenneth Patchen.

Kenneth Patchen, *But Even So*. Copyright © 1968 by Kenneth Patchen.

Kenneth Patchen, *Aflame and Afun of Walking Faces*. Copyright © 1970 by Kenneth Patchen. Copyright © 1970 by Jonathan Williams. This book was first published by Jonathan Williams in *Jargon 6*.

Kenneth Rexroth, *Bird in the Bush*. Copyright © 1959 by Kenneth Rexroth.

Henry Miller, *Stand Still Like the Hummingbird*. Copyright © 1962 by Henry Miller.

Lawrence Ferlinghetti, *Open Eye, Open Heart*. Copyright © 1972 by Lawrence Ferlinghetti.

The author's photo is courtesy of Arthur Knight and his publication *The Unspeakable Visions of the Individual*.

Chronology

1911   Dec. 13, born in Niles, Ohio, to Wayne and Eva Patchen.
       Father was a steelworker and a Protestant; mother was a
       Catholic. The children (one older brother and four younger
       sisters) had a Catholic upbringing.

1915   The family moved to nearby Warren, Ohio, where he
       attended public school.

1928   Graduated from Harding High School in Warren; partici-
       pated in sports, debate, orchestra, and school newspaper.
       First published poems appeared in school poetry magazines,
       two sonnets in *The New York Times*. To earn money for col-
       lege: "Went to work in the steel mill at seventeen."

1929   Attended one year in Alexander Meiklejohn's Experimental
       College at the Univ. of Wisconsin; played track and
       football.

1930   Attended Commonwealth College in Mena, Arkansas, for
       one term.

1930- On the road writing and reading to whoever would listen.
1934   Works odd jobs (migratory worker, janitor, gardener, etc.)
       in U.S. and Canada. In New York City, writing and working
       from 1931–1932; attended writing classes briefly at
       Columbia.

1933   Befriended by poets Conrad Aiken and John Wheelwright
       in Boston. Meets Miriam Oikemus on Christmas Eve in
       Boston.

1934   Married Miriam, June 28 in Sharon, Pa. — All future works
       dedicated "For Miriam." They moved to Greenwich Vil-
       lage, New York, where he worked on the American Guide
       Series, a WPA writers' project.

1936   First book of poems *Before the Brave* published by Random
       House. Received Guggenheim Fellowship; travels to Santa
       Fe, New Mexico.

1937   Patchens lived in Hollywood, California; working on film scripts. "Violent attack of back disability" — Miriam Patchen.

1938 Living in Norfolk, Conn., Patchens worked for James Laughlin's New Directions Publishing. Short story, "Bury Them in God," appeared in *New Directions 1939* collection. *First Will and Testament,* poetry; Patchen is viewed as a proletarian writer.

1941 *The Journal of Albion Moonlight,* pacifist anti-novel.

1942 Working in graphics, originates "painted books," limited editions of books with individually painted covers by the author — *The Dark Kingdom,* poetry. *The Teeth of the Lion,* poetry. "The City Wears a Slouch Hat," radio-play.

1943- Though back injury kept him out of World War II, he re-
1945 mained a loud conscientious objector throughout the war.

1943 *Cloth of the Tempest,* poetry.

1944 Received Ohioana Book Award for *Cloth of the Tempest.*

1945 *Memoirs of a Shy Pornographer,* anti-novel.

1946 *An Astonished Eye Looks Out of the Air,* collection of paci-fist poetry. *Outlaw of the Lowest Planet,* poetry, published in London. *Sleepers Awake,* anti-novel (prose and concrete poetry); *Selected Poems,* revised 1958, 1964; *Pictures of Life and Death,* poetry; *Panels for the Walls of Heaven,* composite of prose, poetry, concrete poetry, and painting. Henry Miller *Patchen: Man of Anger and Light,* first substantial criticism; includes Patchen's "A Letter to God." *They Keep Riding Down All the Time,* prose.

1947 Patchens living in cottage at Old Lyme, Conn. *To Say If You Love Someone,* poetry, printed but not distributed.

1948 *See You in the Morning,* romance novel; appeared first condensed in *Ladies Home Companion;* plans aborted for distribution by Sears Roebuck.

1949 *Red Wine and Yellow Hair,* poetry.

1950 Jonathan Williams transcribes text for *Fables* at Old Lyme. Patchen also does private taping of poetry and fables read to jazz recordings. A Writers Committee formed to raise funds for corrective surgery on Patchen's severely pained spine. Back surgery is temporarily successful.

1950 Patchens are living on Green Street in San Francisco until 1955.

1952 *Orchards, Thrones and Caravans,* poetry.

1953   *Fables,* prose, published by Jonathan Williams as *Jargon 6* in Germany. *The Famous Boating Party,* prose poems.

1954   Received Shelley Memorial Award. *Poems of Humor and Protest,* poetry collection published by poet-friend Lawrence Ferlinghetti. Patchen is working on silkscreen portfolios.

1955   *Glory Never Guesses,* silkscreen folio of poems-and-drawings.

1956- Patchens are living in Palo Alto, Calif., his writing head-
1972   quarters for the remainder of his life.

1956   Spinal fusion gives Patchen new relief and physical freedom. *A Surprise for the Bagpipe Player,* silkscreen folio of poems-and-drawings.

1957   Patchen pioneers with Kenneth Rexroth and Lawrence Ferlinghetti the Poetry-and-Jazz Movement. Tours the U.S. and Canada in club, campus, and concert performances of poetry-and-jazz from 1957–1959. *Hurrah for Anything,* poems-and-drawings.

1958   Recorded *Kenneth Patchen Reads with the Chamber Jazz Sextet. Poemscapes,* prose poems. Recorded *The Journal of Albion Moonlight* (not released).

1959   Recorded *Kenneth Patchen Reads with Jazz in Canada* and *Selected Poems of Kenneth Patchen.* His play *Don't Look Now* was to appear off-Broadway and did appear in Palto Alto. "Surgical mishap" damages his spine and leaves him bedridden and in pain for the remainder of his life.

1960   *Because It Is,* poems-and-drawings; *The Love Poems of Kenneth Patchen,* poetry collection; *Kenneth Patchen Reads His Love Poems,* recorded in Patchen home.

1962   *The Moment,* bound edition of two earlier silkscreen folios.

1966   Pioneers "picture-poem" form in *Hallelujah Anyway. Doubleheader: Poemscapes* and *Hurrah for Anything,* collection.

1967   Awarded ten thousand dollars for lifelong contribution to American Letters by the National Foundation of Arts and Humanities.

1968   *But Even So,* picture-poems; *Collected Poems of Kenneth Patchen.*

1969   One man art show at Corcoran Gallery, Washington, D.C.

1970 *Aflame and Afun of Walking Faces,* fables and drawings; *There's Love All Day,* poems; *Wonderings,* collection of picture-poems and drawings.

1972 *In Quest of Candlelighters,* reprint collection of earlier prose books. Patchen dies January 8 of heart attack at Palo Alto home. Feb. 2, Memorial Reading at City Lights Poets Theater, San Francisco.

1973- Two recordings released, *Patchen's Funny Fables* and
1977 *Patchen Reads from Albion Moonlight.* Art exhibits of Patchen's work — San Francisco Art Institute, Stanford University Library, University of North Dakota.

1976 *The Argument of Innocence: A Selection from the Arts of Kenneth Patchen,* by Peter Veres, art reproduction and interview with Miriam Patchen.

1977 *Patchen's Lost Plays* ("The City Wears a Slouch Hat" and "Don't Look Now").

CHAPTER 1

A Life of Pain and Beauty

D URING the thirty-six years of his writing career (1936–1972) Kenneth Patchen published roughly a book for every year, producing an abundance of solid work and startling innovations. He pioneered experiments in the anti-novel, concrete poetry, poetry-and-jazz, irrational tales and verse, as well as painting and poetry experiments which he termed "painted books," "poems and drawings," and "picture-poems." Through the efforts of patron press New Directions, almost all of his works, including the creditable *Collected Poems* (1968), are still in print. Though Patchen was infrequently anthologized throughout the 1940's and 1950's, during the last decade his works have been receiving new and wider recognition in anthologies.[1]

As a maverick from the academic world, Patchen's highest praise has always come from such diverse fellow poets and writers as Robert Penn Warren and Richard Eberhart or William Carlos Williams and Lawrence Ferlinghetti. For a characterization of the Patchen stance and strength we turn to poet William Everson: "I best see Patchen as one who cocks a terrible right arm against the glass jaw of New York, stunning it with all the contradiction of its values he can summon against it. And if he seems impervious to his passion and his power that is only the deceptiveness of time, for he will survive it, as the power of the poet always survives the metropolis that hates and ignores him in the moment of his accusation. Bless him in his pain and passion, for his cry is heard."[2] It is precisely this sense of passion, beauty, and pain that distinguishes Patchen's life as well as his art, for the two are inextricably one in him.

Patchen's contemporary reputation as poet-experimenter and his relevance to contemporary life are affirmed by younger writers such as David Meltzer: "Patchen's work is a Bible torn out of

17

America's heart. It is the prophet's urgent warning.... Patchen's intense and humane visions have inspired new generations of poets and writers. Like Blake and Whitman, his spiritual forefathers, Patchen's work lays the vital groundwork of man's future."[3] Allen Ginsberg declares that "a new consciousness flowers in youthful U.S. that Whitman, Cendrars and Patchen helped transmit."[4] Indicative of the current reestimation of Patchen's art is Jess Ritter's analysis that "Cummings, Williams, and Patchen were the three between-the-wars poets who most fully explored the possibilities of American poetic language and form."[5] Long extolled by our "underground" art movement, Patchen's present applicability is interpreted by Richard Hack in *Chicago Review* as "Clearly Patchen can easily excite us now for his being a forerunner and nourisher of the 'life culture' ... He knew that mere writing was garbage, ... that phantoms oppress us and possess us, that articulation of the real is all. For this, his good work is universal and lasting."[6] At one time chastized for his formal excesses and personal obscurity, Patchen is now viewed as a social prophet and an artist of extreme "openness" in form.

Kenneth Patchen died of a heart attack January 8, 1972, in his Palo Alto, California home. In the February Memorial Reading held in San Francisco's City Lights Poets Theater, Patchen's deep and lasting influence was recognized in the words and presence of such contemporaries as Robert Duncan, Gary Snyder, Lawrence Ferlinghetti, Charles Lipton, Al Young, Ishmael Reed, and Robert Creeley. Patchen's widow Miriam had instructed Al Young to announce that in a final act of union with existence, Patchen's body had been cremated and the ashes spread upon the Pacific Ocean.[7]

During those thirty-six years of prolific talent, Patchen suffered the physical anguish of a crippling back injury and his mental torment of witnessing the spiritual death of civilization. His work is monumental, however, in its refusal to surrender on man and on man's potential for beauty in the world. In the last years of his life Patchen could reflect: "My case is late T. V. Gothic novels. I don't feel bitter about it. But I'm not particularly resigned to it, either.... I have come to terms with the pain. It's just not occurred to me not to be sustained. I haven't given up hope yet."[8] As a poet of the will, Patchen's work reflects the strengths of his life. Forged in the furnaces of a proletarian youth, Patchen's art and life were molded by an avant-garde and counterculture movement in Green-

wich Village and Connecticut, were recast on the San Francisco
West Coast, and ultimately were tempered and formed in Palo Alto
by an existence of crippling physical pain yet creative beauty and
release.

I *Proletarian Roots*

Hailed as an American proletarian poet of the late 1930's,
Patchen's identification with the life of the poor was hard earned in
the mining and industrial atmosphere of Ohio's Mahoning Valley.
Born to Wayne and Eva Patchen on December 13, 1911, Patchen's
grandfathers had worked as coal miner and farmer-blacksmith. Of
English, Scotch, Irish, and French descent, the Patchens were part
of the early industrial revolution sweeping over Ohio. His father
spent over twenty-five years working in the steel mills of the Niles-
Warren area, and both Patchen and his brother worked for a time
in the mills. With its rows of two story wooden frame houses lining
streets without sidewalks, Niles cradled the early Ohio iron and
steel industry, returning to the immigrant families subsistence incomes and a blanket of smoke and dirt upon their lives. Much like
D. H. Lawrence's mining background in England, Patchen's roots
in a hard working yet culturally wasted community of poor and
semi-poor gave him an early sense of strength and violation. A
sensibility to the cruelty of a powerful capitalism provides the early
chorus for his poetry of protest. Like Sherwood Anderson who
depicted beauty and waste existing simultaneously in Ohio's rural
small towns, Patchen, born thirty-five years later, depicted the
travesty of industrial waste upon the lives of its workers. In "May I
Ask You a Question, Mr. Youngstown Sheet & Tube?" he presents
in searing simplicity some of the aimless profanation of human
potential he witnessed:

> Mean grimy houses, shades drawn
> Against the yellow-brown smoke
> That blows in
> Every minute of every day. And
> Every minute of every night. To bake a cake or have a baby,
> With the taste of tar in your mouth. To wash clothes
>   or fix supper,
> With the taste of tar in your mouth. [9]

Life's choices are held to the daily drudgery of labor, and procreation is viewed as a necessary outlet to the boredom.

Patchen's own home and Catholic upbringing are alluded to in another stanza:

> Bedrooms
> Gray-dim with the rumor of old sweat and urine. Pot roasts
> And boiled spuds; *Ranch Romances* and The Bleeding Heart
> Of Our Dear Lord — "Be a good lad...run down to Tim's
> And get this wee pail filled for your old father now."
>
> (*C.P.* 281)

Over it all is the daily imagery of their lives as they move about in a grotesque form of acceptance:

> Rain dripping down from a rusty eavespout
> Into the gray-fat cinders of the millyard...
> The dayshift goes on in four minutes. (*C.P.* 282)

Though Patchen's art should not be classified as regionalism, an autobiographic sense of places does emerge as a continuing strain in the overall chorus of his work.

Like James Joyce and William Faulkner, writers who both hate and love their environmental roots, Patchen was not immune to the strength and beauty of his youth where even the town's hero, President William McKinley, was the son of a blast furnace operator. His attachment to the people sensitized him to their stark and simple beauty. Recalled as "one of the most beautiful things I know about," he describes:

> When I was five years old my father got hurt
> Very badly in the mill; they carried him in
> Through the kitchen of our house — two men
> At his head, two at his feet — and carted him upstairs.
> The point is this: during the quarter of a century
> My father spent in the mills, never once
> Did he come from work through the front door;
> And the men who brought him home that day
> Took the trouble to lug him in by the kitchen. (*C.P.* 292)

Patchen's relationship with his father, as one of unspoken love and respect, revealed early how suffering could be statuesque. His "Family Portrait" describes how "Great tarry wings splatter grayly up out of the blinding glare of the open-hearth furnaces" as his father arrives home, "washing at the kitchen sink. The grimy water runs into the matted hair of his belly. The smell of scorched cloth and sweat adds its seasoning to the ham and cabbage. The muscles of his back ripple like great ropes of greased steel. An awesome thing to see! Yet he never raised his hand in anger against any man" (*C.P.* 398–399). The life of his father is captured through its common imagery of work and home. Refusing to maintain such stoic silence concerning the human violation of industry, Patchen does, however, inherit his father's strong pacifism. One of the forbears which Patchen claims is Sir Aaron Drake, the British General who deserted the army during the Revolutionary Period to marry a Pennsylvania farm girl — thus setting an early precedent for Patchen's own path of love and peace.

In his early childhood, the family moved to nearby Warren where he, his brother and two sisters received their schooling (two additional sisters died in early childhood). Located only a few miles from Hart Crane's birthplace in Garretsville, Ohio, Patchen began an early apprenticeship to poetry. He published two sonnets in *The New York Times* while quite young, and he proudly admits, "I started a diary in my twelfth year; been writing at something ever since."[11] In an environment that did not pay ready homage to academic ability, he garnered a wide student body respect for his achievements in track and football as well as scholarship and debate. These activities he would continue in his year of college at the University of Wisconsin in the Alexander Meiklejohn's Experimental College of 1929. One of Patchen's Warren classmates, Mrs. Alice McKibben, remembers him as "well liked, but serious and aloof at times."[12] In their special English class, students and teachers readily acknowledged his poetic gift, and his early work appeared in school publications.

To pay for his college education, Patchen was forced into a closer confrontation with the steel mills. Two summers he worked along side of his brother and father in the mills. An early poem recalls:

> the time a friend of mine was picked off
> by a steel fan in the mills back home; it cut him all to
> hell but the rolls didn't stop and nobody missed eating

> at the proper time. I was seventeen and the nightshift
> was pretty hard to take. Not much later I got in on my
> first strike. (*C.P.* 81)

Thus initiated to the accepted violence of human destruction, Patchen's proletarian protest, which soon widened from this regional stance to include people impoverished anywhere by political and economic controls, remained one continuing facet of his varied art. Twenty years after leaving the Niles-Warren area, he could still capture it in a vivid and moving art. "The Orange Bears," which Patchen subtitled on his recording "Childhood in an Ohio Steelmill Town," stands as one of his finest poems and best characterizations of his early life. Using the "orange bears" as a metaphor extremely suited to the lives spent in the orange-red smoke of industrial pollution, he captures his native grounds through his relationship to its people:

> The orange bears with soft friendly eyes
> Who played with me when I was ten,
> Christ, before I left home they'd had
> Their paws smashed in the rolls, their backs
> Seared by hot slag, their soft trusting
> Bellies kicked in, their tongues ripped
> Out . . .   (*C.P.* 384)

His innocence destroyed by the harsh realities of the mill, the poet turns to art as a means of understanding it all. Tracking through the woods with a volume of Whitman, he sits by a polluted stream:

> And I just sat there worrying my thumbnail
> Into the cover — What did he know about
> Orange bears with their coats all stunk up with soft coal
> And the National Guard coming over
> From Wheeling to stand in front of the millgates
> With drawn bayonets jeering at the strikers! (*C.P.* 384)

Patchen's own direction to organized resistance and to the creation of a new art founded in the reality of the now are indicated here. The strength of his passions overruling his sense of artistry is a characteristic of his work, yet one can see here the hidden artistry — the broken line timing, the metaphoric complexity blended with historic detail, and the overriding sincerity creating its own natural and open form, as life and art are wed.

Another revealing aspect of Patchen's early family life was his relationship to his mother. Indicating that she was "a very devout Catholic" and that the children had been raised Catholic, he confesses: "My mother had the thought and hope that I would become a priest."[13] As a poet-priest, Patchen came close to fulfilling that role. Besides being a visionary and prophetic artist for mankind, his essential message is one of universal and personal compassion as mankind's Godhood and salvation. "Career for a Child of Five" is his own explanation for both the flamboyance of his art and his ultimate rejection of a fearful religion:

> My mother got the palms from the hands
> Of the priest himself; and being doubly blessed
> As they were, she would put them on the bureau
> Near candles, where their shadows reeled
> A devil's walk through my childhood. (*C.P.* 110)

Lying in terror and intimidation, the child is compelled to cry out at this pious threat:

> I started to say all the foul words
> That boys had taught me; beginning
> Softly . . . then louder, louder,
> Until mother came and put soap
> In my mouth to rub them away. (*C.P.* 111)

Rather than accept parental models of submissiveness to life, Patchen is lead to a "Career" of cursing at the tactics of terror which he found in the world. He provides this psychological insight to himself and his art:

> And now, when I can't sleep,
> When the shadows bring the boy back,
> It's always he who is able to cry;
> The foul words remain to me. (*C.P.* 111)

If cursing can be a kind of preaching, then this is the priestly method for Patchen's art of protest. His continued and broadened

concern for the proletarian masses is evidenced in his 1966
Hallelujah Anyway where it takes the form of a fiery execration:

> Crazy pigs! Get into the streets and tell them STOP IT!...
> You Judas-paid pissers in the Face of Christ!
> Skins of black, yellow, white — our brothers! I suppose
> the butcher's price is the same — starvation, slavery —
> A-Bombs. Our brothers! this merchandise of death — I suppose
> we should rejoice that the money-changers have been
> driven from our radioactive temples — & coins of flesh
> and blood made the standard of this trade.[14]

Though Patchen was to leave the Niles-Warren area at 18 and
though his family was never to accept him or his rebellion again, he
never forgot the people who had revealed to him man's potential
for demeaning as well as meaningful lives.

II   *An Artist Identity*

Following his successful year at the University of Wisconsin in
1929, Patchen set out in the footsteps of Whitman and Sandburg to
wander the United States and Canada working at odd jobs and
writing continually. Miriam Patchen describes those years: "His
rambles through the country during the depression included most
of the classic jobs and situations of such a life with one notable difference: everywhere, he left behind him sheafs of manuscript: forgotten, overlooked, lost — but he was always creating."[15] Though
he attended Commonwealth College in Arkansas for a semester in
1930, Patchen had turned to the self-educated life of an artist. This
transition in his life is rendered in "The Nervousness of Memory"
as an identification yet necessary break with his proletarian past.
Without glorification he speaks of the ugly cruelty of "these, my
people, / My blood degree" and confesses "they are what I am. /
And what I will not be" (*C.P.* 273). As artist he declares a rejection
of their life pattern: "My native I am to cherish a finer realm"
(*C.P.* 273).

The years 1931–33 included a stay in New York City where he
worked, wrote, and studied writing briefly at Columbia University;
later finding work along the Green Mountain Trail of Vermont. By
1933 he had[16] met and befriended the poets Conrad Aiken and
John Wheelwright in Boston, and there one Christmas Eve, after

three years of such purposeful rambling, Patchen read a poem to a lovely coed from the University of Massachusetts. Miriam Oikemus, daughter of Finnish immigrants, had struggled to pay for a year of college, and, though she had been an early anti-war organizer at Smith College in 1933, she also had come away disillusioned with academic life. Of their first meeting she recalls, "As soon as he read me one of his poems, I knew he was a poet."[16] Their marriage five months later on June 28, 1934, began a lifelong partnership in life and art. Miriam's influence on Patchen's work ranges from that of providing physical and spiritual sustenance to that of embodying the love inspiration for his countless love poems. She explains, "Poetry was our child ... I realized that Kenneth's voice could go much further than mine in supporting causes like the anti-war movement so I helped him in any way I could."[17] Patchen acknowledges his debt by building the Miriam edifice in his work, by dedicating all his works "For Miriam" and by allowing their love to symbolize in his writing a saving force of mankind.

Thrusting themselves into the world of America's avant-garde artists, the Patchens moved into a one room apartment above the Dutch Reformist Church in New York's Greenwich Village. With the exception of a brief sojourn in Sant Fe, New Mexico in 1936 and some Hollywood film writing in 1937, they lived in and around Greenwich Village from 1934 to 1950. With the publication of his first book of poetry by Random House and the winning of a Guggenheim Fellowship in 1936, Patchen was firmly launched on his writing career. *Before the Brave* brought him early acclaim as a proletarian poet as well as comparisons with W. H. Auden and Stephen Spender.

This transition from a working-class youth to an artist is captured in Patchen's story "Bury Them in God" which was published first in the *New Directions 1939* collection.[18] Heavily autobiographical in environment and detail, if not incident, it is Patchen's portrait of the artist as a young proletarian. The narrator-artist is pictured in the Niles-Warren area of his youth as well as the Greenwich Village apartment of his present, where he struggles to "write out" this segment of his life so that he might get beyond it as an artist. Using another character, Swanson, as an alter ego, Patchen presents the two struggling identities of his past and his life as an artist. Miriam, as Mary in the story, is already seen as a consoling force. The artist's struggle to create art from life provides the plot for this story as for all of Patchen's prose works to come. Of particular significance is the writer's revised attitude toward the poor masses, which parallels Patchen's own disillusionment with proletarian mass reform. He shouts down Swanson's liberal rhetoric with: "And where do you come in ... spewing your guts about the working class? ... They'll rise up against their masters ... Sure, they'll rise up, to build a bigger manure pile than they had the last time."[19] Like Patchen, the narrator-artist refuses to glorify the poor, for he recognizes the depth of their bondage: "Look, you bastard, go out in the street and listen to your working class champing at the bit to sink its teeth into the Japanese or German working class."[20] As man and artist Patchen is able to maintain the broadest perspective on social insanity and so makes a moral stand against the greater sin — the destruction of human life. Reflected in this story of 1939 is Patchen's personal and artistic growth, creating an engaged art from the raw material of his life.

If 1936 brought recognition and achievement for the Patchens, 1937 witnessed the initial incident in the progressive debilitation of his health. Miriam reports, "In the fall Patchen's back trouble began as a result of his trying to separate the locked bumpers of two cars which had collided."[21] Patchen's violent attack of back disability was early diagnosed as arthritis, and years of costly cortisone treatment were begun. In crippling pain, Patchen moved about with a cane. Not till 1950 would the problem be correctly diagnosed as a slipped disc and some temporary relief gained through a spinal fusion. Money for the corrective surgery in 1950 would be earned by readings done by a Writer's Committee consisting of T.S. Eliot, W.H. Auden, Archibald MacLeish, Thornton Wilder, E.E. Cummings, Edith Sitwell, Marianne Moore, and William Carlos Williams, among others. In Henry Miller's 1946 *Patchen: Man of Anger and Light* we have Patchen's own estimate of the influence pain played on his writing:

The pain is almost a natural part of me now — only the fits of depression (common to this disease) really sap my energies and distort my native spirit.... Actually (the worst part) is that I feel that I would be something else if I weren't rigid inside with the constant pressure of illness; I would be purer, less inclined to write (say) for the sake of being able to show the sick part that it can never become all powerful; I could experience more in other artists if I didn't have to be concerned so closely with happenings inside myself; I would have less need to be pure in the presence of the things I love, and therefore (probably) would have a more personal view of myself.[22]

As Patchen so candidly confesses, the pain had a crucial influence on his writing, but what may not come across is that this pain could both limit and broaden the expression of his art. As an intimate with suffering, Patchen's reservoir of pain could also serve to amplify his writer's voice. One immediate result of his physical confinement was his turning to visual graphics as a means of expanding his artist's world. Miriam confides that "after a violent attack of back disability in 1937, he found himself forced back to his world of visual-structured creatures."[23] By 1942 he had created his first "painted book" in *The Dark Kingdom* with his own individually painted covers. *Cloth of the Tempest* (1943) contained his early work with "picture-poems," as drawings and words intermix on the page.

Whether living in Greenwich Village, in Mt. Pleasant, New York, or in Connecticut, Patchen was a presence in the avant-garde Village environment which both nourished him and allowed him to nourish others. In 1939 the Patchens were living in the 81 Bleeker Street loft that Herman Melville had inhabited; in 1942 they lived on New York City's Avenue A, and in 1945 on West 12th Street; all the while Patchen is either bedridden or forced to maneuver the Village streets with his walking cane. Harold Norse recalls his first meeting, as a young writer at a Village party, with Patchen: "He possessed great warmth and something else, very rare, that seemed to emanate from his personality like a physical substance: compassion. I thought he looked like an Italian Renaissance master or ancient Welsh bard, maybe. Or even a Hebrew prophet. He was very gentle. With his walking stick (anachronistic, tho necessary), his imposing bulk, massive head and slow movements, he definitely stood out in the Village landscape."[24] The Patchens had established a valuable alliance with James Laughlin, and during 1938–39 lived in Norfolk, Connecticut, as editors of his New Directions Press. Laughlin recalls, "The Patchen's devotions, when the going was very rough, was remarkable.... He, along with Henry Miller, are the writers of his generation whom the alienated young of the underground sub-culture still 'dig' the most."[25] In fact, as Anais

Nin records in her *Diary* for 1940, she was the lone dissenter in a
growing coterie which her close associates Henry Miller and Robert
Duncan had developed with Patchen.[26] His books were coming out
at the rate of one a year, including *The Journal of Albion Moonlight* (1941), his first anti-novel, on which he did both the editing
and assisted on the printing. It was first published through a sub-
scription plan with such notable supporters as Maxwell Perkins,
E.E. Cummings, Wallace Stevens, William Carlos Williams, and
Stephen Vincent Benét. During the war years Patchen was, of
course, not drafted because of his back injury. He was, however, a
loud conscientious objector to all of man's wars, and through his
association with poet William Everson, then serving in a C.O.
camp in Oregon, Patchen published through their press a collection
of his pacifist writing — *An Astonished Eye Looks Out of the Air*
(1946).

Still suffering physical disability, the Patchens moved in 1947 to
their cottage in Old Lyme, Connecticut, where they continued to
offer a haven for young artists who would pilgrimage to their
home. One such writer was Jonathan Williams who nostalgically
recalls, "Kenneth and Miriam Patchen lived in a tiny red cottage up
on a little hill ... past a pond of turtles.... The cabin sat in Connecticut less than it did in the context of many of Kenneth's love
poems. All the neighborhood animals sat on the lawn like heratic
beasts."[27] Not surprisingly, here Patchen would dictate his fabulous creature fables to Williams in 1950, who would see them published by his own Jargon Press. Williams remembers Patchen's
strength then: "His spine at that time gave him no flexibility. Either
he stood or he lay down.... It is the nature of Patchen's imagination that it never sleeps, contemptuous of the obstacles of all the
pain."[28]

In 1950, the Greenwich Village and Connecticut days ended
when the Patchens sought new horizons on the West Coast, but his
influence on the avant-garde world of the East was deeply etched.
In this telling metaphor of the man and his art, Lafe Young presents his own image of the personal stature which Patchen projected on the Village landscape: "Near the wall of one of the rooms
was a very large brass gong. Kenneth was magnetized by this
beautiful gong and before long he was wailing away, whamming
into it with a long padded drumstick. A few of us watched him —

this vital, handsome poet pounding out and in tune with a wild wonderful music."[29]

III   *West Coast Horizons*

The 1950's found the Patchens seeking an expanded view from the West Coast. Taking advantage of his new mobility from the 1950 corrective surgery, the Patchens moved to the North Bay area of San Francisco where he soon befriended Kenneth Rexroth and later Lawrence Ferlinghetti in 1954. Patchen's long line of avant-garde work, his defiance of academia, and his constant anti-war and anti-materialism values made him an immediate artistic presence and influence on the Beat and later West Coast literary movements. Though he denied membership in the San Francisco Renaissance, as he did all regional classifications of his art, he was an established and independent force affecting the culture and artistic climate of the place. Allen Ginsberg recalls a day in 1955 at the City Lights Bookstore when Ferlinghetti first introduced him to Patchen: "I had published *Howl* through City Lights, and Patchen was a senior survivor of the poetry spiritual wars who'd kept his verse-line open, spontaneous, and his heart in human body. He looked like a mild longshoreman, with a hat, slight painful smile, perhaps even low voice... I was surprised to find him living so near the center of literary S.F., so available and friendly."[30] Patchen later declared contempt for the hypocrisy of the Beat Movement, which Ginsberg co-founded, for at least two reasons. First, he had published sixteen books by 1950, and though the Beats brought him new acclaim, in the face of critical stereotyping he had to fight for his artistic identity. Secondly, his philosophy embraced some of the Beat rejection of materialism and capitalistic controls; however, it ran antithetic to any spirit of Beat or "hipster" nihilism.

Patchen was truly "there," and his presence in San Francisco enlivened the whole place. By 1955 he had published *Poems of Humor and Protest* as number three in Ferlinghetti's historic Pocket Poets Series. Further experiments in combining writing and graphics resulted in the silkscreen folio editions of *Glory Never Guesses* and *A Surprise for the Bagpipe Player,* "poems and drawings" of 1956. That same year he gained new relief and further physical freedom from a second spinal fusion, and by 1957 he used his new mobility to launch with Ferlinghetti and Rexroth the whole Poetry-and-Jazz Movement.

Patchen's efforts with poetry-and-jazz will be analyzed more closely in a later chapter; however, some biographical chronicling can be sketched here. By 1956 the Patchens were living in Palo Alto on the southern end of the San Francisco Bay near Stanford University. This home became his artistic center for the remainder of his life. Though Patchen, Ferlinghetti, and Rexroth had all experimented with the synthesis of poetry and jazz, it was not until 1957 that they sought to publicly perform their art. Ferlinghetti and Rexroth opened at The Cellar club in San Francisco, while Patchen opened at the Black Hawk. Appearing with the Chamber Jazz Sextet, Patchen began a tour of concert halls, night clubs, college campuses, and television shows. In his identifiable scarlet blazer, Patchen toured the U.S. and Canada in 1958 and 1959 appearing at such universities as British Columbia, California at Los Angeles, Washington at Seattle. In August of 1958 he propagated the poetry-and-jazz experiment on Bobby Troup's televised "Stars of Jazz." Following months of record breaking performances at Los Angeles Jazz Concert Hall, Patchen carried poetry-and-jazz to New York's celebrated Five Spot Cafe and made his first recording for Cadence Records — *Kenneth Patchen Reads with the Chamber Jazz Sextet.* While his play *Don't Look Now,* a jazz drama, was to appear at off-Broadway's Living Theater in 1959, he was working with jazz great Charlie Mingus. Vancouver, Canada, was the scene of a 1959 radio performance and recording with the Alan Neil Quartet — *Kenneth Patchen Reads with Jazz in Canada.* In three years, poetry-and-jazz had progressed from a strange new phenomenon to an exciting aspect of music and literature, and in the process it attracted a new and broader audience for the brother arts of jazz and contemporary poetry.

In the midst of this activity and acclaim, Kenneth Patchen experienced a personal tragedy and an appalling setback. In a final 1959 back operation, further exploratory surgery was prescribed. Following the spinal operation and before exploratory surgery could begin, what was termed a "surgical mishap"[31] occurred. Patchen had slipped from the operating cart to the floor severely damaging his spine. Further surgery was cancelled, and Patchen was sent home to Palo Alto to a bedridden life of pain.[32] These new limitations to Patchen's horizons brought initial disillusion and depression, but were met finally by his courageous will to live and his ever expanding consciousness.

IV   *Palo Alto Days*

In 1960 and 1961 to help the Patchens financially, for in addition to his medical bills Miriam had developed multiple sclerosis and could not work, William Packard organized a series of fund raising tributes in coffee houses, clubs, and campuses around the country. Climaxing in the reading at San Francisco's Marine Memorial Auditorium in January, 1961, Kenneth Rexroth served as master of ceremonies with readings by Jonathan Williams, Philip Whalen, Michael McClure, and Lawrence Ferlinghetti. Despite this support from San Francisco Renaissance figures, Patchen drifted further and further from his earlier literary friends, cutting off a life he could not have. In a rare interview in 1967, Doublas Dibble describes Patchen's state: "He lay sprawled across the double bed on his left side, his head propped up with his left hand. A pair of glasses were shoved up over his forehead and into his wiry hair."[33] Though Miriam describes the 1960's as a time of "total confinement to home, hospitals, doctors, writing and painting,"[34] it was also marked by surprising productivity. Before his "surgical mishap" Patchen made recordings for Folkways of his *Selected Poems* and of sections from *Albion Moonlight*. Refusing to abandon performing, he recorded at his Palo Alto home in 1959 and 1960 *Patchen's Funny Fables* and *Kenneth Patchen Reads His Love Poems*. His authoritative *Collected Poems* was published in 1968, and a one man exhibit of his art was held in Washington D.C.'s Corcoran Gallery of Art from December, 1969 to January, 1970. Paintings, painted books, picture-poems, and concrete poetry were exhibited. Patchen's wry humor capturing life's irrational network and bizarre circumstances produced the final volumes of *Because It Is* (1960), *Hallelujah Anyway* (1966), *But Even So* (1968), and *Wonderings* (1970). Confined to his four walls, he turned increasingly to his theme of the ready wonder inherent in the world and in man's internal consciousness of it.

Miriam Patchen describes the Patchen world during the last twelve years of his life as "physically torturous for him since he [could] not sit, lie on his back, or move more than slightly without incurring monstrous pain, painting little words on paper [gave] him

air from the cramped bedroom, everything else, including the page,
close[d] in.''[35] Patchen's compulsion to create would not be cur-
tailed by mere circumstances, no matter how severe. He explains,
''My working periods vary. Some days I can manage 15 minutes to
half an hour. Other days it's several hours before I get knocked
out .... Yes, it's compulsion. I've never stopped writing since I
was 12.''[36]

Refusing to allow others to witness his suffering periods,
Patchen's friends, nevertheless, did not forget his talent nor their
debt. In 1967 he received for his lifelong contribution to American
letters a ten thousand dollar award from the National Foundation
of Arts and Humanities. Two close friends who were intimate with
Patchen's Palo Alto world recall those final years of creating
beauty despite the daily pain. Norman Thomas remembers the bedroom studio with its ready mixture of paint brushes and writing
tools and how ''at midmorning his face is grey and the lines at the
side of his mouth are deep, his eyes sunken and dark with miserable
night memories. When he moves it is with so much care and with
such apprehension. For all his nights are long; all his sleep is
troubled.''[37] Despite this anguish, James Boyer May reveals the
ultimate insight that ''Patchen's restraint is finally seen to be a
shield, a cloak for a sensitive inner self.... The central key to his
character lies in his love for all that lives: plants, animals,
man...and stars.... He is a teacher, too.... For he teaches by his
chosen *ways* of being.''[38]

At the time of Patchen's death in January of 1972, his reputation
as an American avant-garde artist was well established, and it continues to broaden as the fruits of his formal experimentation are
gathered by his contemporaries. At the Memorial Reading at City
Lights Poets Theater the following month, Morton Marcus
explained, ''When a poet dies, it is important that other poets
gather and chant,''[39] and so artists who had been touched by
Patchen's life and art paid a final tribute. Kenneth Patchen's influence on his contemporaries has emerged as a model of a life and
an art united in its witness to the anguish and beauty of living, for
as May explains, Patchen ''hears, sees, and feels the noisy flux as
well as the far music and visions — and those formless forms of ...
silence.''[40]

CHAPTER 2

A Vision of Life and Art

CHARACTERIZED by its abundance, its social relevance, its extreme individuality, and its formal innovations, Kenneth Patchen's art demands a radically new criticism. While academic critics have contented themselves with either avoiding Patchen's work or forcing it into distorting categorical classification, this study is based on the premise that Patchen's radical independence as an artist requires an individual approach. An understanding of the form and function of Patchen's work can only be gained through a recognition of his personal vision of life and art.

Though Patchen is a visionary and not a philosopher, three pervading and felt principles underlying his world view and controlling his art can be identified: 1) "man's madness" — the estrangement of man from his true life through the corruptions of violence, state, and materialistic controls, the inhumanity of man, and an insane conditioning by society; 2) "engagement" — commitment to life through love, brotherhood, and a belief in the unity of life; 3) "wonder" — an innocent, free, and imaginative response to the world's beauty as the ideal approach to life. Within this desperate yet vital view of life, Patchen's theory of art is "functional." His art is designed to both reform and form man by forcing a recognition and consequent rejection of "man's madness" and by demanding an "engagement" in the true life of "wonder." Following William Blake's vision of the poet as prophet and priest, Patchen creates an art whose chief function is the saving of mankind from itself. Combining a realistic appraisal of existence with Romantic ideals of life, he ideally becomes the prophet and forgotten conscience of mankind and a creator, through his art, of a radically new human consciousness. A description of Patchen's vision as a critical launching place is thus imperative for an understanding of his art.

33

Following related ideals of the master creator "total artist" whose life and art are one, and the independently controlled and created "total book," Patchen incorporates a mixture of media within his art, seeks to perform his art upon his audience, and works for an expanded and rejuvenated view of art based on its affective results. As a poet of the will, he is a model of the contemporary engaged artist. His pragmatic aesthetics, based as they are upon the affective results generated within the audience, thus lead to the creation of his protean experimental forms.

In defining an artist's vision, one risks distortion if he denies it development. Patchen's own vital concern for growth is reflected in his world vision, which develops according to a pattern of shifted emphasis within his tripartite and consistent view of madness, engagement, and wonder. Raymond J. Nelson's study of "American Mysticism: The Example of Kenneth Patchen" parallels Patchen's development with the mystical path, progressing from the Illumination to the Purgation to the Union.[1] In reality, the developmental pattern in Patchen's world view is not this linear and clearcut, but is a series of shifting interrelationships. These relationships broaden in meaning and shift in importance: first, "man's madness" immediately broadens in meaning from the controlling insanity of institutions and power to the irrationality underlying all of man's societal behavior; second, "engagement" shifts in emphasis from an involvement in social reform (viewed now as futile) to a commitment to personal reform and salvation; third, the concept of "wonder" remains consistent in meaning but receives primary emphasis in later works, emerging as Patchen's central theme. Recognizing that any assessment of a philosophical development oversimplifies, it is provident to acknowledge here the complex pattern of interrelatedness that does appear. Patchen's overall image of the world, however, remains clear; it is man's pathway within that world that changes. Believing that man's madness is all too apparent and that engagement in mass social reform leads to corruption and ultimate futility, Patchen turns in his late writings to man's potential for wonder as his best and only alternative.

Playfully employing the titles of poems, often satirically, obliquely, or even with disdain for audience comprehension, Patchen's use of titles for his books is another case entirely. These are given the significance of overall statements of the book's

message, and thus they can immediately suggest Patchen's shifting world vision. His initial work, *Before the Brave* (1936), sounded a proletarian challenge to the workers against those in power, but it is followed by the broader and more human issues of *First Will and Testament* (1939). The chronicle of man's destruction is recorded in *The Journal of Albion Moonlight* (1941). By 1946 his concern had become that of a desperate forewarning to all of mankind, viewed now as *Sleepers Awake on the Precipice* and lamented as *They Keep Riding Down All the Time.* By the 1950's he had shifted completely from organized social reform to a realization of personal imaginative wonder, which he celebrates in titles *Hurrah for Anything* (1957), *Because It Is* (1961), *Hallelujah Anyway* (1966), *But Even So* (1968), and ultimately a book of *Wonderings* (1971). These titles, indicative of free celebration, also acknowledge the world's chaos and the necessity of turning from it. They are celebrations of life despite the gaping abyss man has dug for himself. Such an overview of Patchen's art must be completed with a close analysis of his vision and the experimental art created to fulfill it.

I   *An Individual Art*

Whether it was by virtue of his proletarian roots, his underground artistic associations, or his unceasing and uncompromising quest for radically new forms, Patchen's art received relatively little critical attention. Another contributing factor was the literary scholar's reluctance earlier in the century to deal seriously with defiant and radical experimentalists. This position of the avant-garde artist against the academic world and thus against critical scholarship is something Patchen himself encouraged. Literary critics and liberal intellectuals often appear in his works as villainous do nothings, as people apart from the concerns of real life. His parody of the educated critic, Mr. Brill, in *Memoirs of a Shy Pornographer,* reveals his own estimation of his relationship with critics. The scene is a cocktail party, and Patchen discloses his tone by entitling this chapter, "The Last Party I Ever Went To":

"And Patchen?" she asked, pencil poised.

"Oh, Patchen — nobody takes him seriously," one of them said. "He's just a rough-neck who never grew up."

"He's just a boring child — a lot of noise about nothing," another said.
"Patchen missed the boat," Mr. Brill said.[2]

His attacks could, of course, be more direct, and under his fiery
cursing also came the aloof critic, the poet who listened to critics,
the money oriented publishers, and a simple minded and obedient
public. In *Sleepers Awake* he protests:

> I think the moaning outsounds the tinkle
> of fat sticky little bards
> who twang their navels in the orderly and
> empty drawingrooms of "Our Literature" —
>   I am so full of rage!
>   I am so full of contempt for these smug lice!
>   I tell them to stay away from my books!
>   I want to stand outside their blood-
> drenched "culture"![3]

Patchen's defiance of critical aloofness was encouraged by the
reviews of fellow poet experimentalists and friends. Rexroth has
protested the treatment of Patchen's work as "A conspiracy of
silence of the whole of literary America."[4] Jonathan Williams
terms it "A collective turning of the backs and shifting of the asses.
Nothing very organized, simply the unionized apathy, jealous dis-
interest, and niggardly behavior of literary drones."[5] Though the
existing lack of critical response to Patchen's work does lend some
credence to these accusations, it is well to remember that the radical
nature of his theme and form impeded scholarly treatment of his
work. He certainly runs antithetic to the New Critics of that time.
The point, however, to be recognized is that Patchen has suffered
from this long critical rivalry. Willing to be a martyr for any cause
he believed in, he may have martyred his art to years of undeserved
obscurity.

A second problem in approaching Patchen's works is the distorting oversimplification fostered by criticism bent on "placing" him
in a literary movement. Labels such as proletarian, surrealist, beat,
and mystic belie his true range and motive.

As early as 1940, when American criticism was awakening to the
curious phenomenon of the proletarian writer, Patchen was hailed
by Amos N. Wilder as "the American proletarian poet."[6] Comparing him with Muriel Rukeyser, Charles I. Glicksberg labeled him "a

fullfledged proletarian poet for whom revolt is a spiritual necessity."[7] Though proletarian themes run strongest in Patchen's early
books, even there they are only one element of his art, as an
examination of the richly complex *First Will and Testament* readily
reveals. Henry Miller's 1946 study, *Patchen: Man of Anger and
Light,* though heavily laced with biographical impressionism,
added a recognition of the dualistic character of Patchen's art, seeing him as capable of great tenderness as well as blistering social
protest.[8]

By the 1950's the surrealistic aspects of Patchen's works were so
prominent that Glicksberg reappraised him as a surrealist, or, more
accurately, as a failed surrealist. This 1952 summary of his work
forced Patchen into the surrealist mold and then found his writing
"Surrealism run amok."[9] Though Glicksberg is a revealing critic,
he distorts one aspect of Patchen's writing for a general characteristic. Similar dadaist comparisons are best seen as just that — analo-
gous descriptions.

Perhaps the most detrimental label placed upon Patchen has been
that of "Beat." Linked by geography, associations, and influence
with the San Francisco Renaissance of the late fifties and sixties,
Patchen, like Lawrence Ferlinghetti and Gary Snyder, had to spend
much time and temper disclaiming the Beat label. In the early misunderstanding of the Beat movement, anthologizers tended to
stereotype anyone who read poetry to jazz as Beat. Although
Patchen partially sympathized with the Beat poets' rejection of academia and of a materialistic and violent society, he opposed "hipster" nihilism, and naturally resented the restriction of his twenty
years of writing to an inappropriate label. His antagonism grew
until he struck out at the hypocrisy in the movement, calling them
"A Freakshow worth every Madison Ave. penny of the three-
dollar-bill admission."[10]

Most recently, Raymond J. Nelson has attempted to follow a
Whitmanesque strain in Patchen's work.[11] His study places Patchen
at the heart of an American mysticism movement, but here too the
categorical labeling of "mystic" mars the insights of this scholarly
treatment.

Certainly, revealing insights have been made into Patchen's
methods, among them Frederick Eckman's assessment of the essential Blaken character of Patchen's vision and William Carlos Williams's startling analysis of *The Journal of Albion Moonlight.*[12] It

was Kenneth Rexroth, however, who directed new attention to other aspects of Patchen's writing: his love poetry, his anti-war writing, his drawings and poems, and his fables.[13] Aligning Patchen's art with international counterparts in Paul Eluard, Henri Michaux, and Wyndham Lewis, Rexroth offered valuable insights into the anti-literature methods, particularly the methods of madness which Patchen used functionally as a curative mirror of social insanity. However, the criticism stands generally as slanted, scattered, and sparse.

To a unique degree, Patchen, as man and artist, provides the truest source to his art. His conjoined view of life and art reveals the form and function of his works. Harvey Breit's early analysis of "Kenneth Patchen and the Critical Blind Alley" first recognized the inescapable sense of Patchen's personal and individual manness that so controls his art: "Kenneth Patchen's poetry is a last testing of the critic's seriousness. In Patchen the poem's tension is not in the quantities and measurements where the critic is safest, but in what is human: in hate and love, in what men remember and in what men dream, in what they must get.... The critic is pretty much by himself, thrust out into an intensified and heightened, but very real, world. He must say something — as a critic and, more, as a responsible man."[14] The critic is forced to abandon literary clichés and go to the heart of the work — Patchen's bold and vital view of life and art.

William Carlos Williams explains the source and authority by which Patchen creates: "There is no authority evidenced in this but the man himself. If there are others like him, if we are not all somewhat as he is, provided he write truthfully and out of a gifted mind, he has a right to speak and needs no other authority."[15] Not literary polish, but the capturing of personal and universal truth is the authority for Patchen's art. James Dickey cautions us on this requisite expanded view for Patchen: "He is a poet not so much in form as in essence, a condition of which we should all be envious, and with which we should never be satisfied. To evoke the usual standards of formal art in Patchen's case is worse than meaningless."[16] It is clear that Patchen's vital view of life and his functional view of art are at once his poetic "essence," and the critical key to understanding his works. The critic Breit advocates this approach to Patchen:

What is required for an understanding of Patchen's poetry is an understanding into the creative process itself. And by this process is meant, too, what it feeds upon, that is the multitude of sources, the values and beliefs, the time, the pastness in it, the credible things and the outmoded things, above all, the sums of these which...the poet must create for himself. If for no other reason, Kenneth Patchen's poetry is of significance for us because it reveals more sensitively, more truthfully, the poet's function.[17]

It is precisely this interrelated vision of his role as man and poet, as the poet-prophet for his age, that offers the critical pathway to illuminating Patchen's works.

II *Patchen as Poet-Prophet*

"I am a poet of life,"[18] declares Patchen's narrator-hero-persona in *Albion Moonlight*. Not an uncommon claim for any artist, Patchen elaborates on the extreme degree to which his view of life will affect his art: "You will be told that what I write is confused, without order — and I tell you that my book is not concerned with the problems of art, but with the problems of this world, with the problems of life itself — yes, of *life itself*" (*Albion,* 200). The desperate needs of this life — where Patchen saw man's violence and insane greed precluding a life of love and wonder and advancing man to the threshold of destruction — control his art. The role of the forgotten, insistent, and prophetic conscience of mankind is the task he takes on, and voices in "The Hunted City":

> My Poem will be building in the blood of young men
> and I shall remember what they have been forced
> to forget.
> There is a desperate task here. (*C.P.,* 163)

As poet-prophet to man, Patchen offers a message, nevertheless, directed and founded in the reality of the *now*. If it is a forgotten conscience, our recognition of it makes it more emphatically our own. His *Panels for the Walls of Heaven* contains his prayer to poets descriptive of the state of the world and the artist's new function within it:

> O my poor lost brothers if any of you has poems to write
> write them now O if any of you has anything to add to the

long tall dignity of human creation please add it now O if
any of you has a pure heart let that heart beat in praise of
God for O my brothers the world is dying and we will not
let it die.   (*C.P.* 348)

The artist must meet the world's dying with his belief in the divinity
of human life, and through the action of his committed art restore
vitality to that life:

> TO FORGIVE IS TO UNDERSTAND
> ART IS GIVING
> THE SAVED MUST SAVE THE REST![19]

It is just this sense of imperative action and spiritual mission which
dictate Patchen's functional aesthetics and his concern for redefining the artist's role in society. His long surrealist drama-poem
"THE OLD LEAN OVER THE TOMBSTONES" closes with his
impassioned self-image of the poet-prophet: "I sing for the flame
and against the ever-grinning darkness" (*C.P.* 95).

In an art so dedicated to the visionary function of presenting the
world as it is and as it should be, it becomes essential to delineate
Patchen's perception of the present world. What are the characteristics of his world view that will shape his art? We must recognize
at the start that Patchen is not a "philosopher," that he is not concerned with presenting a complex system of thought, but with por-
traying accurately his felt reaction to the world. His world view is
not theorized; it is beheld. We admire, not its intricate complexity
of thought, but its searing frankness and consistent moral stand.
Kenneth Patchen's vision of life is surprisingly simple and constant.
Underlying all his work, it frequently rises to the surface as a desperate appeal expressed in a radical form, and, at other times,
issues forth as an open attempt to communicate.

Man is the center of Patchen's world, and therein lies all the hope
and all the blame. In *The Journal of Albion Moonlight,* Patchen
has his narrator state simply, "Our message was this: we live, we
love you. Our religion was life" (*Albion,* 17). In one of the poem
prefaces to *The Dark Kingdom* he states metaphorically the same
theme, "Life's end is life.... Your native zone is silence; everything you want is within you. Do not seek the ungranting fire; man
himself is the flame" (*C.P.* 247). Such idealism concerning man's
potential was conditioned by the reality which Patchen saw around

him, yet he refused to accept things as they were or to blame them on an Absurd existence. It is a man centered theism that he preaches in "Red Wine and Yellow Hair":

> Come cry come in wrath of love and be not comforted
> Until the grave that is this world is torn asunder
> For human the lock and human the key
> O everything that lives is holy!
> And Man and God are one in that mystery. (*C.P.* 404)

Patchen's consistent reference to God, puzzling to many readers, is best understood as directed to the divinity he found in man, and not to the traditional Christian concept. His "A Letter To God," first published in 1946, leads to this conclusion: "Believe in man. Belief in man is God."[20] Glicksberg summarizes well Patchen's compelling human theology: "Patchen cries: *We must learn to live for the first time.* That is his categorical imperative: Man as God must learn to worship himself and the murder in his heart must be torn out by the roots."[21]

Patchen's ironic sense of the social absurdity which man has created despite his divine potential leads to the "Anger and Light" dualism which Henry Miller observes in Patchen's works. "I know of no American who has as vigorously insisted that the enemy is within. . . . He knows that the enemy of man is man. He rebels out of love, not out of hate."[22] Such a compassionate rebellion is confirmed in a letter which Patchen wrote to Miller, "It's always because we love that we are rebellious; it takes a great deal of love to give a damn one way or another what happens from now on: I still do."[23] A man centered world where God is in man, a universe of unimaginable potential and an absurdly futile reality, characterize Patchen's vision of life. "A hundred thousand no ones / With just themselves to blame, not God."[24]

To attribute an existential or Absurdist outlook to Patchen is a mistake, for the absurdity he finds is in the insane waste man has brought into the world, not in an insane or absurd existence. Viewing himself as a voice in man's irrational wilderness, Patchen is best approached as one who holds before man the mirror of his wrongs. Like Molière and the true Camus, he is a "moralist" of his times. His concern for the larger circle of mankind is expounded in *Albion:* "Let me explain: we all of us live in many worlds, worlds

made up of the color of our skins, the size of our noses, the amount
of our incomes, the condition of our teeth, our capacity for joy,
pain, fear and reverence, the way we walk, the sound of our voices;
and there is above these little worlds another world which is common to all men: the world of what is everywhere on earth'' (*Albion,*
305).

In this larger universal world Patchen recognizes the mad and
wrongful influences of man. He once observed to Henry Miller, "I
wish they'd give me just one speck of proof that this 'world of
theirs' couldn't have been set up and handled better by a half-dozen
drugged idiots bound hand and foot at the bottom of a ten-mile
well."[25] This perception of the world molds his art into a prophetic
warning. Of the irrational method of systematizing mankind he
alerts us in "Sure There Is Food":

> *There is eating one's self . . .*
> The way you've got it made
> Everybody is mad after while
> Then you can come up with a world
> Where madness is the normal thing . . .
>
> This world's the best example I know. (*C.P.* 343)

In his prose Patchen's indictment of social insanity often takes the
form of direct statement: "It's crazy to believe, is it? Let me tell
you that it exceeds the wildest insanity to accept some of the things
which the world takes for granted—" (*Memoirs,* 176–177). Thus
"man's madness" is an essential element in Patchen's vision; basically he believes that "There is no danger from the world; all that is
dangerous lives in us" (*Albion,* 83). As poet-prophet Patchen must
confront us with this madness in his art, forcing us to recognize and
reject it.

Against this dark vision of the world as it is rests Patchen's pervasive idealism concerning human potential — the world as it
should be. He concludes *Albion Moonlight* with the assurance that
"There is no darkness anywhere. There are only sick little men who
have turned away from the light" (313). Ingredients in the "light"
he speaks of include the key visionary components of "engagement" and "wonder." They encompass a belief in love (including
the sexual); a belief in brotherhood, which embraces an everyman
concept based on the unity of life; a belief in faith as essential to

life; and a belief in an open and freely imaginative response to the world's beauty.

Patchen uses a platform speaker in *Memoirs* to preach the basis of his belief: "To love all things is to understand all things; and that which is understood by any of us becomes a knowledge embedded in all of us.... To recognize truth it is only necessary to recognize each other" (87). Love and brotherhood are put in the larger perspective of that common world which we all share, the unity of all life. A little further on he explains, "One who speaks the truth shall eventually and inevitably outsound the world; and one who lives the truth shall have a life in everyman forever" (*Memoirs,* 89). This belief in speaking the truth for the universal everyman is thus the basic motive of Patchen's visionary art. The seeming paradox of Patchen's being a poet of both protest and love, which he shares with E. E. Cummings, resolves itself when his love of mankind is seen as the motive for his protest over the needless sacrifice of human values. In his only conventional novel, *See You in the Morning,* the idealism of his vision is openly expressed: "Clouds. Trees. Grass. These are beautiful things. The wonder of life is in them. Life's holiness.... In Brotherhood, live — or, blind and without faith, we shall all go down into darkness together."[26] In the Romantic tradition of Wordsworth, Emerson, Thoreau, and Whitman, "wonder" is affirmed as a transcendent force pervading all existence. One does not analyze the world; one beholds it with open childlike wonder. This engaged response to life Patchen characterizes as "Humbly — but without caution (in unbridled vigor of faith: acceptful of joy for whatever reason, for no reason — humbly I believe!) ... In the serene and beautiful prevailation of life, from causes beyond understanding, I believe!" (*C.P.* 459).

Against this suggested background of a man centered theism, Patchen, aware of man's irrationality and committed to restoring his lost ideals, presents his prophetic message. His art is a testament to the ultimate reformability of each man. As Miller accurately observes, "Setting himself apart from the world, as poet, as man of vision, Patchen nevertheless identifies himself with the world in the malady which has become universal."[27] Before considering how Patchen's art directly fulfills his tripartite world view, it is necessary to understand his individual and functional aesthetics. Just as his art is devoted to restoring meaning to life, Patchen's continuing

concern for redefining the role of the poet today is deeply embedded in his writing.

III   *A Functional Art*

As part of the desperate means to deal with a desperate world,
art is used by Patchen as a functional tool. It therefore must be
dissociated from traditional views of art that would limit it to its
asocial aesthetic value alone. Because Patchen views art as a pragmatic tool in an era of spiritual emptiness, he shows little concern
for writing about "Art" for art's sake. One rare exception is the
brief introductory declaration in "The Hunted City" printed in the
1939 *First Will and Testament* and later reprinted in the *Naked
Poetry* anthology of 1969, as if to say this is all I have to say about
craft.[28] This scarcity is indicative of his disdain for those who idly
indulged in art worship, and suggests the anti-art, anti-literature,
direction of his works. "How much better the world would be without 'Art'" (*Albion,* 19), his narrator concludes, the quotation
marks and capitalization of "Art" are significant. He would write
art, and it would be a tool used to save mankind, not a glorified
tradition. Patchen's aesthetics and poetics must, therefore, occur
within his writings as functional observations or as demands and
directions toward redefining art and reestablishing the artist's role.
Like the Surrealists and Dadaists, and like Henry Miller, Patchen
debunks traditional "Art" in favor of a more vital "art."

Returning to John Dryden's classic *An Essay on Dramatic Poesy,*
quoted in "A Note on 'The Hunted City,'" Patchen explains the
need for new and more living forms. Dryden speaks against the
stagnation of traditional "Art" forms: "There is scarce an humor,
a character, or any kind of plot, which they have not used. All
comes sullied or wasted to us: and were they to entertain this age,
they could not now make so plenteous treatments out of such
decayed fortunes. This therefore will be a good argument to us,
either not to write at all, or to attempt some other way."[29] Using
Dryden as an established tool against "Art" and in justification of
avant-garde innovation, Patchen is declaring his own artistic
mission to "attempt some other way." He expresses Dryden's
sentiment with more color when he proclaims through Albion,
"Our images are fat with the grease of old caves where madmen sit
thinking out new horrors — our art, religion, society ... where is

the sunlight!'' (*Albion,* 27). Like Blake, Patchen believes that man has been corrupted by the language of images and symbols of the past. The false and limited icons of ''art, religion, and society'' must be thrown off. ''I am telling the truth. Man has been corrupted by his symbols. Language has killed his animal'' (*Albion,* 15) is the complaint of *Albion Moonlight,* Patchen's most profound book on art and society. As the long list of his experimental forms testifies, there is in Patchen a driving compulsion to 'make it new,' to advance the guard of art into striking forms and broadened relevance.

A second characteristic of Patchen's functional aesthetics is his compulsion to go beyond ''Art'' by openly confronting the reader with direct communication. Glicksberg describes it as Patchen's breaking ''into the prophetic, ejaculatory strain, as if his heart can no longer contain itself and leaps beyond the confines of art.''[30] This drive toward direct confrontation Glicksberg correctly attributes to the fierce urgency of the message: ''This explains the nature of his creative purpose, his religious motive. He is trying to make light shine in the universal darkness. He would do without the protective and distorting garments of Art.''[31] Patchen's methods are necessarily severe; as Henry Miller explains, ''Patchen uses the language of revolt. There is no other language left to use. There is no time.''[32]

In *Albion Moonlight,* a chronicle of the allegorical pilgrimage of a band of individuals in a world gone mad with violence, Patchen employs the perceptual double exposure as the reader watches a novelist writing about a novelist writing. This technique operates functionally to explore the nature of the artist's stance toward his art and toward the pragmatic and insistent demands of life. His narrator-self breaks into open expression of narrative consciousness within the personal atmosphere of journal writing: ''They will not really listen because at times I became afraid and tried to clothe my spirit in Art; but I was a fool to think this — they can *feel* me coming out at them'' (*Albion,* 23). Not only must the artist make it new, he must use any means necessary, regardless of conventional ''Art'' standards, to affect and engage his audience. ''In art there is ever the demand for the distorted, for an indefinable thing termed 'magic.' But for the artist, there can be only one distortion: that which is not art. To say it another way, the world is in a mess precisely because a bunch of stuffy fools insist that there be no mess''

(*Albion,* 120). It is well to remember here and elsewhere that Patchen's own definition of "art" and the "mess" provide the truest understanding of his works. It is the "stuffy fools" defining "Art" who refuse "art" and ironically perpetuate the world's "mess." The Dadaist parallels are striking.

Patchen's art is at once functional and creative, for he seeks to generate new forms to create a new world. "The great writer will take a heroic stand against literature: *by changing the nature of what is to be done*" (*Albion,* 308), and for Patchen no less than a world resurrection dictates the change required. In curing this sickness of the world, Patchen requires that the artist maintain personal integrity and avoid political propaganda: "It is my belief that in a troubled age like ours the poet can be of service only if he permit no half-truths indigenous to political maneuvering to obscure his own deepest convictions and instincts. Poetry is inimical to the lie — whether it be a 'good' lie or a 'bad' lie."[33] Besides his independence and honesty, the artist is viewed here in "service" to a "troubled age." This is the position Patchen adopts for himself and for all true artists. As poet-prophet for this age he declares, "I speak for a generation born in one war and doomed to die in another."[34]

Patchen's answer to what the artist should do is, of course, revealed in the art he made; however, it is also the subject of a long and important statement on the artist's duty outlined in *Albion Moonlight.* Printed on the page with two other messages in the juxtaposed and simultaneous printed form characteristic of Patchen, it nevertheless can be isolated and revealed as Patchen's manifesto as an artist. He begins by describing the artist's stance toward life and his audience:

> So it is the duty of the artist to discourage all traces
>   of shame
> To extend all boundaries . . .
> To establish problems
> To ignore solutions
> To listen to no one
> To omit nothing
> To contradict everything
> To generate the free brain . . .
> To tinkle a warning when mankind strays
> To explode upon all parties

> To wound deeper than the soldier
> To heal this poor monkey once and for all.
>
> *(Albion,* 253)

Using the action form of the infinitive, Patchen suggests the kind of engaged involvement required of the artist today as he moves from daring individualism to acts of generating, exploding, wounding, and finally the overall metaphor of healing. The action of wounding is the immediate precedent to that of healing, suggestive of Patchen's method of attacking his audience so that he might cure them. He clarifies the artist's world involvement:

> To inhabit everyone
> To lubricate each proportion
> To experience only experience. . .
> To extend all shapes. . .
> To exclaim at the commonplace alone
> To cause the unseen eye to open. . .
> To raise a fortuitous stink on the boulevards of
>   truth and beauty. . .
> To lift the flesh above the suffering
> To forgive the beautiful its disconsolate deceit. . .
> To flash a vengeful badge at every abyss. (*Albion,* 253–255)

Revealed as a universal presence, the artist is involved in the "commonplace" of life, and in awakening the "unseen eyes" of the world. The "fortuitous stink on the boulevards of truth and beauty" directly suggests the provocative but necessary anti-art which he must make. His art then becomes the "vengeful badge" flashed at the lying abyss of nihilism and despair.

A final look at this song of the artist reveals a sharp focus on the artist's own personal involvement:

> To *happen*. . .
> It is the artist's duty to be alive
> To drag people into glittering occupations. . .
> To assume the ecstasy in all conceivable attitudes. . .
> To blush perpetually in gaping innocence
> To drift happily through the ruined race-intelligence
> To burrow beneath the subconscious
> To defend the unreal at the cost of his reason

> To obey each outrageous impulse
> To commit his company to all enchantments. (*Albion,* 255)

One ultimately arrives at the path of wonder that Patchen so perpetually followed. Forcing his readers to realize the "glittering occupations" of imaginative joy through wonder, he drifts happily in the "gaping innocence" of ideal childhood. To achieve this state Patchen suggests burrowing into the repressed "subconscious" and obeying "each outrageous impulse." His dualistic mission is suggested in his leading to a positive world of "all enchantments" while also requiring the artist "To peel off all substances from the face of horror" (*Albion,* 256). Though laced with deliberate ambiguity and presented in the outraged chaos of the simultaneous poem form to tone down its didactic directness, this poetic statement of the artist's duty in a troubled age stands as a clear guide to Patchen's art and world vision.

The interrelationship of Patchen's view of life and art are thus contained in his image of the poet-prophet's role. In a direct address interjected in *Albion Moonlight* he defines Albion's and his own artistic role: "The reader will remember that A. Moonlight is not a reformer, nor an informer, an outformer, an underformer nor an overformer; he is a *former*—savvy?" (*Albion,* 143). Respecting no insular customs in his attempt to awaken mankind, the artist begins by forming an art which in turn will leave his audience "formed" as well. His involvement in life is not on the level of an instructor (an "informer") but on that of a poet-prophet who would rejuvenate the reader and thus the world through his art. In a glimpse at the artist's ultimate function Patchen sums up much of the misunderstanding of his own artistic mission: "The function of the artist is to express love. What most people fail to understand is not the artist's work, but his essential unworldliness in wanting to give love."[35]

CHAPTER 3

An Art of Madness

PATCHEN'S diagnosis of the insanity of mankind is written across the pages of his works. To cure it, he prescribes an initial confrontation of our sickness, "peel off all substances from the face of horror" (*Albion,* 256). This facial metaphor for the horror is one which Patchen uses in his earlier surrealist drama-poem "AND IN ANOTHER PLACE USES THE SAME PHRASES" where the persona-artist Mr. Kek answers the young girl's objection to his ugly "frog's face leering at everybody and everything" with the defensive explanation, "My face is what it sees" (*C.P.* 120). Patchen's art, like Mr. Kek's face, is a reflection of what he sees — the accepted mania of mankind. This madness — chaos, violence, and irrationality — of Patchen's art remains one of the chief areas of misunderstanding. Recognizing the basic functional design of his art to save the world, one must also discern a method of madness used to save it.

Like a psychiatrist, Patchen would force a shocking confrontation with reality to awaken man. Believing that a bold recognition of the insanity would be followed by a consequent rejection, Patchen turns the madness upon itself. It was William Carlos Williams' review of *Albion Moonlight* which first revealed this therapeutic treatment: "What virtues are to be found here may be taken for madness. Could we interpret them we should know the cure. That is, I think, Patchen's intention, so, in reverse, to make the cure not only apparent, but, by the horror of the picture imperative."[1] This is the critical path which Kenneth Rexroth follows in his analysis of Patchen as the "Naturalist of the Public Nightmare." Recognized as a *recorder* of the world's insanity, though some might disagree with the accuracy of his vision, Patchen's covert and curative method underlying his handling of madness is not generally recognized. Speaking of the "mass psy-

49

chosis," Rexroth defines Patchen's treatment of it: "Patchen turns it upon itself, dissociates its elements, and uses them to create a vast, controlled, social dream, a diagnostic symbol of the collapse of civilization."[2] Not merely a reporter, Patchen is revealed as an artist deliberately making art as it has always been made, to broaden man's consciousness.

We need then to measure the boundaries of Patchen's mad world. Three aspects of "man's madness" which receive most of Patchen's concern are capitalistic materialism, human violence, and an absurd conditioning to accept the social insanity. His portrayal of society is tempered by the madness he perceived, as he himself observes, "The sickness of the world probably didn't cause mine, but it certainly conditions my handling of it."[3] Glicksberg describes Patchen's world as "a wild beast run amok, its fangs dripping with blood, intoxicated with the smell and taste of blood. He is filled with uncontrollable hatred for the cant and cruelty that rules modern life.... This world of ours is portrayed realistically as a museum of horrors, every room of every house haunted by the spectre of war."[4] Patchen's description of society captures the horror he perceives. As Rexroth explains, "The nightmares of Patchen's narratives are the daily visions of millions."[5] War and capitalistic materialism are two nightmare realities which Patchen witnessed.

Though Patchen associated with Leftist thought of the 1940's and 1950's, he was an independent thinker and not part of a movement, communist or otherwise. As a spokesman for proletariat concerns throughout his career, Patchen's sympathies grew naturally from his experiences in a small Ohio steeltown. Though *The Journal of Albion Moonlight,* his strongest social statement, advocates *"establishing a world-wide Socialism"* (90) as a social-political cure, Patchen's concern is primarily diagnostic. He wants chiefly to expose the madness of the existing capitalist system. His advocacy of an ideal Socialism grows out of his compassionate brotherhood and is later conditioned by a disillusionment with the inherent evils of all existing social movements. World War II, the explosion of an atomic bomb, Stalin's corruption by power with Soviet Communist dominance of its satellite countries, together with the proletarian support of the war were all factors in Patchen's later rejection of group social reform. His revolution is internal and non-violent. "Capitalism and Fascism are one under the iron mask.... War is the life blood of Capitalism" (*Albion,* 90). In his open protest, these two maxims are vigorous denunciations reflecting his deeper concerns for brotherhood and human compassion: "Do you understand this? Your backs are bent under the junk of property, which you came by because of your fear. You were afraid to possess your soul, so you went by the wayside and acquired property. It has been said that property is theft: I say that property is murder. The hands of dying children reach up through your bread" (*Albion,* 25). He goes on to explain the complicity of capitalism and war: "Your dollars become rifles: you will protect with the last drop of somebody else's blood what was never yours. You walk on my face. I am the poor. I am the one in whose house you live. It is my food you eat" (*Albion,* 25-26). The real focus of Patchen's treatment of capitalism lies with the insane destruction he reads in the distorted values and lives of his brothers.

Aware of the perpetuating process of man's conditioning to madness, he warns, "it's not what happens that frightens us ... it's what it does to us" (*Albion,* 84), and ultimately that "we protect ourselves by going mad" (*Albion,* 84). For Patchen, the malady appears most blatantly in our sacrificing of real life, in our dying into the "life-lie." He warns:

> What is madness if not this world?
> Aren't all their evils a kind of madness!
> Is it sane to lie when the lie kills?
> Is it sane to accept evil when that evil brings death?
> Is it sane for man to murder himself!
> Why should we kill each other?
> WHY SHOULD WE KILL EACH OTHER![6]

Revealing the physical as well as spiritual murder committed on and by mankind, Patchen exposes a self-destroying lie that has become life today. Miller sums it up as "THE WAY MEN LIVE IS A LIE! — that is the reality which screams from the pages of these books."[7]

In rejecting social movements and institutions, Patchen asks instead that each man awaken from the insanity that blinds and controls him to the sanctity of all life. Thus we are lead to a consideration of a related madness — human violence. In 1945 Patchen pulled his earlier poems on war together with several new ones in

An Astonished Eye Looks Out of the Air. Printed in a West Coast
conscientious objector's camp, the book's preface makes "a few
flat statements"[8] that summarize the basic pacifist belief manifest
in his works:

> I am opposed to all war.
> I don't believe human beings should kill each other.
> I am opposed to all violence — *for whatever reason.*
> I believe that wars will only end when men refuse to
> murder one another — *for whatever reason.*
> I believe these things as a man and as a revolutionist.
> For I believe wars will only end when the present
> murderous forms of society are allowed to die — and
> all men are at last permitted to live together as brothers.[9]

The obvious frankness and simplicity of this moral stand accentuates by contrast the complex rationalizations for war. In an
uncompromising refusal to accept any form of man's violence
(even to revolutionize change), Patchen becomes our "forgotten
conscience" calling to mankind to awaken from a world where war
has existed continuously throughout recorded history. His poems
are thus filled with the grotesque images of "the present murderous
forms of society," as machine guns, tanks, bayonets, bombs, and
corpses crowd his verse. In "I DON'T WANT TO STARTLE YOU
but they are going to kill most of us" he describes a grotesque menu
of war, colored with images of slaughter:

> The General paused to enjoy the floorshow:
> On a raised platform little groups of people stood.
> Flags told their nationality; orators told them what to do.
> As the bands blared they rushed at each other with bayonets.
> The dead and dying were dragged off and others brought on.
> Sweat streamed from the orators; the musicians wobbled
>   crazily.
> The Big Shots were mad with joy, juggling in their seats
>   like monkeys.
> And they never get wise the General said. (*C.P.* 156)

In Patchen's mad imagery of war, he attempts to awaken his
readers from their accepted predatory war values. These values are
stated boldly for man to realize: "Humanity is a good thing. Per-

haps we can arrange the murder / of a sizeable number of people to save it'' (*C.P.* 170). At times Patchen's protest breaks into an open appeal, a kind of shouting from the borders of madness:

> Don't fight their war!
> Tell them to go to hell!
>
> This isn't a poem. This is a sob and a death rattle.
> Who will listen? who will care? (*C.P.* 159)

Patchen's lifelong commitment to pacifism, which rang true for a later anti-war generation in America, views war as essentially a means for the powerful to manipulate the weak through destroying life. Any acceptance of this system becomes for Patchen an insane validation of global irrationality.

As a curative measure, an accurate and vivid expression of universal madness emerges as a molding force in Patchen's art. He opens his *Collected Poems* by urging reality upon his patient — ''Let Us Have Madness Openly.'' Insisting upon a reality confrontation, this important poem compels us to ''follow / The footsteps of this slaughtered age'' (*C.P.* 1) suggesting both violence and controlled sacrifice. Identifying the life and death borders of ''Time's dim land'' where the lives we have led meet ''With the face that dead things wear—'' (*C.P.* 1), our life recognition is given cosmic proportions. The realization at our death is of the old forgotten wish:

> We wanted more; we looked to find
> An open door, an utter deed of love
> Transforming day's evil darkness. (*C.P.* 1)

This idealism of love and concern which might have preserved some of life's essence has been sacrificed to the reality of accepted madness, captured in the closing images:

> We found hell and fog
> Upon the earth, and within the head
> A rotting bog of lean huge graves. (*C.P.* 1)

In this combined image of death and madness one finds not a

fatalistic surrender, but the basic realization and challenge which Patchen places — *Before the Brave*. How he went about molding an art to treat and cure this insanity becomes the next consideration as we examine what may be termed Patchen's "methods of madness."

The experimental forms that Patchen devised to capture this feel of madness, primarily the anti-novel and irrational verse, will be discussed later. Two other "methods of madness" which can be suggested here are the use of a mad imagery of violation and the presentation of structural incoherence through irrationality of cause and effect. Alex Comfort refers to Patchen's hard and grotesque images as "sadistic . . . because in the world we live in they have covered everything, even the flowers, with blood."[12] Patchen seeks to instill precisely this sense of a horrible profanation of life in his audience through his almost surreal imagery. In his early poems the imagery is often used to depict the terrible effects of violence, as in "AND HE HAD WILDER MOMENTS" where he describes the bombing of a village:

> Rats gnaw at the dead.
> Filmed over, eyes, world, music.
> Mozart flaking open to the flies
> What voluptuous graves they have here. . . .
> *Why are they moving that gun up?*
>
> Maggots skate into the castle through silt of kings.
> Oh no, not the Queen lying in her own dirt!
> Notice the lovely rings on her plump fingers.
> My eyes watch all the other eyes, warily. (*C.P.* 108–109)

This grotesque image of 1939 was calculated to bring home the realization of war — forcing Americans to confront the gruesome consequences of their support of the war as well as the devastating results of the bombardiers' acts. Intellectual or strategic distancing from the consequences of war is cancelled in this head-on confrontation of the horror. An expressionistic sense of fear and hidden terror characterize this type of naturalistic detailing.

In "Elegy for the Silent Voices" Patchen's nightmare reality emerges from the description of a ship's explosion:

> and it all going God-high,
> town, engine room, skipper, cripples, spotted dogs,
>   with a diamond
> of thunderous sound, splitting the sky up like a fat
>   fish's belly)
> (People hurry along like pictures taken through milk). (*C.P.* 101)

Through common objects projected in images of violation — the fish's belly splitting the sky — Patchen captures the unspeakable horror of war's events. It is a blurred and numbing sensation of life's nightmares captured in a film of milk. With Freudian agility he senses and releases our subconscious, concluding this poem:

> Behind shouting trees the figure glides like blood
>   in a mouse's side
> Within our faces the poor move their awful hands
>   in desolate proverbs
> Jesus Joseph and Mary it is not thus, it is not thus,
>   it is not thus
> That the whole round world is broken. (*C.P.* 101)

A hard and violated, common imagery of a mouse's bleeding side or the hands of the poor drives home this *feel* of madness. Like Kafka, Patchen creates sensory images of guilt which reach up from our subconscious etching themselves into our awareness.

A second reflector, used to convey the basic irrationality underlying all of man's social behavior, is Patchen's general use of incoherence and incongruity of event and form. His poem "In Order To" from *The Famous Boating Party* captures man's absurd acceptance of the world where every insane event has an equally insane cause:

IN ORDER TO

Apply for the position (I've forgotten now for what) I had to marry the Second Mayor's daughter by twelve noon. The order arrived at three minutes of.

I already had a wife; the Second Mayor was childless: but
  I did it.

Next they told me to shave off my father's beard. All right. No matter that he'd been a eunuch, and had succumbed in early childhood: I did it, I shaved him. (*C.P.* 437)

Combining a satiric portrayal of man's blind acceptance with an absurd sense of the matter of fact insanity of incongruity and incoherence, Patchen treats his audience to a dose of the madness. The demands for the "position" are afterall the common demands of a mad world. After the character in this poem is led to "burn up every man-made / thing on the face of the earth" he is given the ultimate absurd command to "put it all back the way it was when you started" (*C.P.* 437). Both character and Patchen walk away from such a demand, for it is a better world that both would make.

In one of his most characteristic works of the irrational, *Because It Is,* Patchen posits a world where the absurd cause and effect are matter of fact. The title, which ironically pretends to explain the cause of anything and everything, answers the world with a reflection of the incongruent chain of events which comprise present existence. In *"BECAUSE* HIS SISTER SAW SHAKESPEARE IN THE MOON,"* for example, the main absurd character of the book — the little green blackbird — discovers the cause of war:

> So he had some cards printed and
> Handed them out. This of course started
> A war, because the cards were printed
> With ink. And the little green blackbird
> Arrived in Portugal not only without cards,
> But without a head, or arms, or legs,
> Or even a little toe.[13]

There is nothing symbolic about the cards used here; rather, the whole book captures and symbolizes the condition of modern man where absurd event and cause coexist and where no questions are asked.

Patchen's methods of madness will be examined more closely in the analysis of his development of the anti-novel, "picture-poems," and his own irrational tales and verse forms. We can, however, note here as one of the primary functions of his art, the recognition and consequent rejection of man's madness. Turning the insanity upon itself in hopes of restoring health, Patchen creates his own methods of irrationality in imagery, structure, and ultimately experimental forms.

CHAPTER 4

An Art of Engagement

"I am the world-crier, and this is my dangerous career.... I am the one to call your bluff, and this is my climate" so declares Patchen in the poem "EARLY IN THE MORNING" (*C.P.,* 160–1). Out of the searing necessity of the world's condition, he adopts the symbolic position of a pied piper to mankind. Of Patchen's committed art Harvey Breit observes, "It removes action from the sphere of rhetoric and sophistic conveniences."[1] Preaching a complete involvement in and a whole hearted dedication to *life,* Patchen calls man to the action of making a better world, one in which belief is essential to life, every action and inaction has its effect on the life of all men, and love is the primary emotion. In a rare interview, for *The Outsider* magazine, Patchen helps to define this basic theme of his art as "the ascendency of person out of chaos and non-being through feeling, through love."[2] In an art thus dedicated to engaging man and leading him away from madness to light Patchen seeks to embody his vision of life in his art. The primacy of an emotionally engaged art is asserted in *Sleepers Awake:* "Writing is a kind of loving — when the wreath touches your heart,"[3] and in *Hallelujah Anyway* where he suggests, "Feeling I must remind you, is the poet's sign."[4] Envisioning poetic creation as demanding total engagement from both artist and audience, Patchen seeks the functional goal of creating engaged and engaging art.

Before considering his artistic methods of engagement, it is necessary to delineate Patchen's meaning and handling of the engaged state. In his early work one notes through the biting comments of his poems a satiric attack on the evils of inaction, complacency, and apathy; one poem is dedicated to the apathetic as an "Elegy for the Silent Voices and the Joiners of Everything" (*C.P.* 100), and another is presented on the "Eve of St. Agony or the

Middleclass Was Sitting on Its Fat" (*C.P.* 104). In "Street Corner College" the invective is more serious as he laments our half-hearted lives where "We shall probably not be quite dead when we die. / We were never anything all the way" (*C.P.* 74). His "State of the Nation," which he was fond of reading to jazz, depicts civilization in the "HURRY UP PLEASE ITS TIME" barroom atmosphere of T. S. Eliot's *The Waste Land.* World politics are discussed amidst beer drinking and lustful carousing, all of which climaxes in the apathetic conclusion of Patchen's sarcastic overstatement:

> No one knew just why it happened or whether
> It would happen ever again on this fretful earth
> But Jack picked up his beer again and Nellie her beer again
> And as though at signal, a little man hurried in,
> Crossed to the bar and said Hello Steve to the barkeeper.
>
> (*C.P.* 75)

Characterizing the world as a barroom full of overstated inactivity, Patchen, never content to merely lament, protests loudly this disengaged waste of life. His morality is founded upon the contemporaneous question, "Do we know another guilt / than waiting?" (*C.P.* 3).

I   *The Necessity for Belief*

Belief, Patchen's answer to man's apathy, constitutes a basic assumption of his world view and a central theme of his writing. Social insanity is to be met with strength and persistence:

> Aye now is the time to believe
> When there is nothing to believe in!
> Aye, now is the time to believe
> If it does no more than show we're still alive! (*C.P.* 357)

Patchen stands in sharp opposition to any form of nihilism, whether Neitzschean or Beat hipster. In *Memoirs of a Shy Pornographer,* a surrealist saga of the misadventures of detective writer and innocent Albert Budd, he presents a scene where Albert and his crippled lover Priscilla test their faith. By believing in the "green deer," Priscilla, symbolizing mankind, is able to walk.

Speaking for Patchen, Albert explains to her and to us the difficulty yet the absolute necessity of believing:

> Why shouldn't you think it's crazy to believe in a
> green deer? All your life you have been taught to
> believe in only what you can use — to set on the table,
> to put in the bank, to build a house with. What possible
> use would a green deer be to anyone? Who would believe
> in a man with a blazing bush in his cart? Then let me
> tell you that it is beliefs such as these that are the
> only hope of the world. Let me tell you that until men
> are ready to believe in the green deer and the strange
> carter, we shall not lift our noses above the bloody
> mess we have made of our living. (*Memoirs,* 176)

In Patchen's world a belief in faith itself is rejuvenating and man's only hope. It is the root of his engagement. Elsewhere Patchen clarifies what there is for man to believe in, what the green deer can be.

"I sincerely believe that devotion is possible. The hymn is still to God" (*Albion,* 142), Patchen asserts in reaffirmation of man's divinity. Later in *Memoirs* he explains in bold type: "EVERYMAN IS THE GOD WHO STANDS BEFORE YOU" (170). This belief in the universal everyman is clarified in *Sleepers Awake* where he relates it to a unity of life principle: "I thought that there must be a wonderful, central life from which the lives of all creatures had their flowing. Perhaps in this was God" (55). Following the Romantic and transcendent vision of Blake, Emerson, and Thoreau, Patchen recognizes a pervading unity in life that relates all things in a common bond. "You, the woman; I, the man; this, the world: / And each is the work of all" (*C.P.* 72), he asserts of this world where "Anyone who live stand in one place together."[5] From this recognition of the shared life where "All things are all things"[6] springs life's wonder as well as man's brotherhood and his responsibility. Everything is affected by everything else — thus the categorical imperative for engaged action. Sanity and identity could be restored through realizing this brotherhood of life, whereas "Whosoever plots against his neighbor, loses that sense of personal identity which threatens the foundation of your world" (*Sleepers,* 180).

If significance can be attached to an author's final statement, the concluding picture-poem of Patchen's last work is revealing of his underlying belief: "Everyone is me, . . . I am Everyman and he is in and of me. This is my faith, my strength, my deepest hope, and my only belief."[7] More than an assertion of responsibility, through this belief the significance of each man's actions is enhanced by his part in the whole of manhood, and thus Patchen's belief in life has a foundation in experience. We *are* already engaged to each other and life; we need only realize this bond to give life and our lives importance and meaning.

II   *An Essential Love*

In Patchen's world view the essence of engagement is love, presented as man's true state and as a fundamental reality:

> I'll tell you what it is I'm sure of —
> Neither of deathless souls nor fleeting clay,
> But that we're most alive when we love! (*C.P.* 378)

This love can take the form of a compassionate brotherhood, as in his assertion that "There is only one power that can save the world — / And that is the power of love for all men everywhere" (*C.P.* 330), or it can take the form of a sexual-spiritual love between man and woman. That Patchen is a poet of love is readily acknowledged by his critics. Glicksberg remarks on the "two leitmotifs that appear in his work[:] . . . his expressed horror of the chaos and intolerable cruelty of our civilization with its organized techniques of mass-killings, and his courageous affirmation of the transcendent will to love as a binding, redeeming force."[8] Patchen's salient stance toward the power of love is described by Richard Hack: "Most important is love. This is an uplifting emotion, the basis of comradeship, a source of happiness. It is a silent circle of security among the screams of war."[9] Though critics acknowledge the love theme of Patchen's work, little has been done to relate it to other elements of his vision, to madness and wonder.

Love is viewed by Patchen as man's strength, "Power is in living clean before our love" (*C.P.* 34). It is a condition of our engaged essence, "To be is to love" (*C.P.* 189), and it is the source of our awareness of life's unity, "To love all things is to understand all things; and that which is understood by any of us becomes knowledge embedded in all of us" (*Memoirs,* 89). As the essence of any belief and a prerequisite for an active engaged life, love is affirmed in simplistic finality, "Beyond love / there is no belief."[10] Patchen views sexual love as a protective rejection of the world of man's madness. It restores sanity and balance to the distorted life fostered by civilization. One loves in spite of man's world, and that simple and courageous act of loving is made all the more meaningful as man's social actions spiral down toward madness.

In the many love poems Patchen wrote, including the "For Miriam" dedications of all poetry volumes and the collected *Love Poems of Kenneth Patchen* in book and record form, sexual love is given cosmic proportions. Similar to D.H. Lawrence and Sherwood Anderson, Patchen views sexual loving as an essential right of mankind — the act of love is the highest act of living. He warns in "The New Being" of the impending loss threatened by man's social insanity: "Your birthright, liferight / Deathright, and now your / Sexright, you've lost" (*C.P.* 364). Though his most explicit descriptions of sexual love are in *Albion Moonlight,* the sexual act is implicit in all his love poems.

In "I'd Want Her Eyes to Fill with Wonder" Patchen reveals his characteristic approach:

> I'd want her eyes to fill with wonder
> I'd want her lips to open just a little
> I'd want her breasts to lift at my touch. . .
>
> I'd want her thighs to put birds in my fingers
> I'd want her belly to be soft and warm as a sleeping
>   kitten's
> I'd want her sex to meet mine as flames kissing in a
>   dream forest. (*C.P.* 332)

Simplistic and direct sensualism is united with a transcendent spiritual affirmation, as we see in the final image of "flames kissing" amidst the background of "a dream forest." Angels usually surround the sexual act of love, and images of peace and unimaginable communion often substitute for physical detail, as in "AS SHE WAS THUS ALONE IN THE CLEAR MOONLIGHT":

> so when she lay beside me
> sleep's town went round her

> and wondering children pressed against the high windows
> of the room where we had been...
>
> thus does the circle pull upon itself
> and all the gadding angels draw us in
> until I can join her in that soft town where the bells
> split apples on their tongues
> and bring sleep down like a fish's shadow. (*C.P.* 67)

In images of bells, children, and the town, one is reminded of the love poetry of E. E. Cummings, particularly of the classic "Anyone Lived in a Pretty How Town" written the year after Patchen's poem. Most like Cummings is the use of unimaginable, almost surreal, images to invoke the transcending spiritual quality of the act of loving, where one finds "wondering children pressed against the high windows." As two of America's leading love poets, Patchen and Cummings create a modern Romantic imagery — individual, uncommon, and imbued with their shared belief in the spiritual reality of love where, as Cummings expressed it for Patchen, "love is the every only god."[11]

In Patchen's works love emerges as a developed statement on the condition of life. His ultimate rejection of this life of madness in affirmation of a real and whole life of love is described by William Carlos Williams: "And of it all, says Patchen, perhaps the only really normal and good thing remaining is the sexual kiss of two bodies, full fledged."[12] In Patchen's view, one must love despite the world and also because of it. His "SHE HAD CONCEALED HIM IN A DEEP DARK CAVE" reveals the shelter love provides from man's insanity:

> Warm houses stand within us
> Sleepy angels smile in doorways
> Little jeweled horses jolt by without sound
> Everyone is rich and no one has money
> I can love you Thank God I can love you. (*C.P.* 61)

Any escapist overtones of such love statements are tempered by the honest and desperate awareness of life which Patchen builds into the poems. In one of his best known love lyrics "23rd Street Runs into Heaven" the madness, love, and God are all related. Two lovers come in from the streets where "newsboys / Begin their murder-into-pennies round," and they engage in the simple and direct act of two lovers "Who have lain long with their lover" (*C.P.* 112). A mature wisdom is reflected in Patchen's one line judgement of life and love: "Our supper is plain but we are very wonderful" (*C.P.* 112) The whole poem is characterized by its calm matter of fact tone asserting love's secure primacy. Facing the world's horror, love gains strength as a positive and cognitive assertion of a better life — as the essence of engagement.

His rejection of apathy and call for a commitment founded on a belief in the unity and divinity of all life led to Patchen's ideals of brotherhood and sexual love. In *Sleepers Awake,* he summarizes much of his belief in bold type:

THEY TOLD ME YOU COULDN'T BELIEVE. I SAID YOU COULD. I SAID A PERSON COULD BELIEVE IF HE GOT TO KNOW HIS CAPACITY FOR BELIEF—NOT THINGS TO BELIEVE IN, HELL NO, BUT HOW MUCH OF THE THRONE HE COULD GLIMPSE IN HIMSELF, AND HOW WILLING HE WAS TO LET HIS BROTHERS (HOWEVER ROTTEN AND EVIL) SIT ON THAT THRONE. IT'S A LONG WAY TO MORNING, BUT THERE'S NO LAW AGAINST TALKING IN THE DARK. (14-15)

Man's throne is his human divinity; his sharing of it is his recognition of the unity of all life. The brighter morning is sought by Patchen through an art of engagement, one designed to demonstrate and create involvement.

III *Personalism of Style*

"Art is not to throw light but be light. . . . Nothing can happen from the outside" (*Sleepers,* 268). Artist and art must be models of engagement, demanding of man what they demand of themselves. This stance is more than theorizing about aesthetics for Patchen; it is the functional goal for the action of his art. It is just this commitment and demand which Henry Miller recognizes in the degree to which Patchen's art sought to *be* light: "Each new volume is an increasingly astonishing feat of legerdemain, not only in the protean variety of the text but in design, composition and format. One is no longer looking at a dead, printed book but at something alive and breathing something which looks back at you with equal astonishment. Novelty is employed not as seduction but like the stern fist of the Zen master — to awaken and arouse the consciousness of the reader."[13]

Although all artists have sought to present life in their works, Patchen requries more — that his art *be* life or that it demand the creation of life from his audience. Thus, Albion asserts, "There can only be one action: what a man is.... I write this book *as an action*" (*Albion,* 261). His art requires and becomes by example an engaged action of author and reader. Miller's analogy to the "fist of the Zen master" is an apt one, one repeated by other critics who have been struck by Patchen's art. "Work of this kind ... has an impact which is wholly immediate — one cannot evaluate it and read it at the same time. Patchen ... has brought the perfection of this immediacy to a point at which, when it succeeds, is very like a blow in its total effect."[14] Though Patchen would draw us with his lyrical poetry like a pied piper, the severity of the times often requires a rougher awakening.

Raymond J. Nelson compares Patchen to a prizefighter: "Patchen uses his anti-literary tools much as a boxer uses his jab: to test the reader's defences, to weaken them, to keep the attention occupied while a literary haymaker is in preparation."[15] Nelson finds some precedent for this kind of forced engagement in the tradition of Walt Whitman's "Song of Myself" and such avant-garde work as Henry Miller's *Tropic of Capricorn*. He adopts Whitman's term "personalism" to describe this method of engagement in their art — an eccentric embodying of the artist's self in his work demanding a personal involvement of the reader and writer.[16] Whitman had coined the term in *Democratic Vistas* where he pleaded for an American literature of involvement and strong personality in answer to the corrupt and dying American conscience. Wayne C. Booth analyzes this technique in *The Rhetoric of Fiction* under the heading of "distancing," which suggests the degree of difference or closeness in the values of implied author, narrator, characters, and reader.[17]

Patchen's design is to diminish the moral, emotional, and intellectual "distance" between the life of author, narrator, and reader. The functional intent is, of course, to force a breakdown of his audience's acceptance of society's mad values and to lead to a logical and emotional acceptance of engagement. As well as embodying his strong personality in his work, Patchen repeatedly suggests openly the personal and physical closeness he would demand. He asks of his readers, "There are buildings falling. I am cold. Put your arms around me" (*Albion,* 13). He would touch us. The distance separating life and art also comes under attack, as when he breaks off the text with the request to "Put this book aside a couple hours and go out and do something nice for somebody" (*Sleepers,* 87). Through their involved act of reading, Patchen's audience is led into an involved relationship with life. This functional demand of his art for engagement resulting in a personalism of style can also be demonstrated as a molding force in the experimental forms which he created. Through his creative and committed stance as an artist, as well as through the functional design of his works, Patchen creates an art of engagement. His art must be measured by its affective impact upon the reader.

IV   *The Total Book — The Total Artist*

Two related corollaries are engendered from Patchen's art of engagement. First is a concept of the "total book," a belief that the finished product must be, as much as possible, the work of one man. In an effort to sustain the original purity of his vision and creation and to demonstrate his total "engagement" in his art, the artist must take an active part in the creation of the complete book — from writing to printing to cover design. Second, there is a concept of the "total artist" requiring the artist to commit himself to providing a personal model of engagement and wonder. The "total artist" is one with his life and art; his life is a part of his art; above any narrow genre distinctions, he is a master-creator and performer; he seeks to involve his audience in the art of engaged life.

One of the primary unexplored relationships between Kenneth Patchen and William Blake is their shared vision of the "total book." Patchen writes in his introduction to Blake's *Book of Job:* "Blake dreamed of 'the beautiful book' — written, decorated, engraved, printed and illuminated by one creator."[18] It is a dream which Patchen shared, as we find him admitting: "I have, as much as I could manage, had a hand in the design of all my books."[19] Patchen confesses here much more than a passing interest in the final form of his books; he speaks of an ideal goal of his art. In addition to the pages of picture-poems, the books of handwritten poems (Patchen's last three books are virtually devoid of typescript), and his painted covers for special editions, Patchen is also a

careful taskmaster over the publishers and printers of his books.
Henry Miller tells of Patchen's relentless work with the typography
of *Albion Moonlight, Sleepers Awake,* and other works: "How
interesting, too, are the typographical arrangements which he dictates for his books! How competent he can be when he has to be his
own publisher! (See *The Journal of Alibion Moonlight.*) From a
sickbed the poet defies and surmounts all obstacles. He has only to
pick up the telephone to throw an editorial staff into panic. He has
the will of a tyrant, the persistence of a bull. 'This is the way I want
it done!' he bellows. And by God it gets done that way."[20] Following Blake's model of the artist who maintains the purity of his
vision, Patchen is thus involved in all aspects of creating and producing his art. For Blake and Patchen, a "beautiful" or "total"
book is above all a model of engagement and wonder, capturing
both the artistic involvement and the personal sense of marvel
necessary for the creative act.

Just as Patchen's relationship to Blake is revealed in their shared
vision of the "total book," so his relationship to the surrealists is
evidenced through their shared concept of the "total artist." This
kinship with the surrealist movement has remained a troublesome
and ambiguous area of Patchen's art. Whereas Glicksberg finds
Patchen a failed surrealist because he exercises too much conscious
control over the irrationality of his art,[21] Rexroth warns that
"Patchen must be distinguished from the later orthodox
surrealists,"[22] and it is a warning worth taking. Though the surrealist and earlier Dadaist Movement held much in common with
Patchen, he is simply not a surrealist. He has used and defended
surrealist methods: "It is clear to me that when the reader has
digested 'The dog ate the cheese and the small boy in the yellow
coat coughed' he has embarked on no mean adventure."[23] Yet
Patchen has indicated a flat refutation of the philosophy of sur-
reality: "There is no such thing as super-reality. (The surrealists
have managed to put on a pretty good vaudeville act for the middle
class; *but there isn't a religious man among them.*)" (*Albion,* 307).
This spiritual denunciation (strikingly similar to his defensive protest against the alleged sham of the Beats) comes at the close of
Albion Moonlight where narrator, author, and reader are drawn
closest in values, and therefore it must be given credence as
Patchen's own. Peter Veres helps to clarify Patchen's kinship and
struggle with the surrealists, "By the late thirties Surrealism had

become something of a fad, a veneer of styles and effects, practiced by a large group of lesser artists and writers, though its initial masters still continued their work. Patchen seems to reject this cult, yet his work shows his indebtedness to the spiritual concerns of Surrealism as well as to some of its artistic techniques."[24] While "classifying" Patchen as a surrealist leads to confusion and distortion, a close examination of their parallel and shared visions is both necessary and mutually revealing.

Following the favored surrealist approach of analogy reveals the following shared relationships between Patchen and the Surrealists. Despite the fact that Patchen doubted the surrealists' faith in "surreality," it is a post-Romantic concept strikingly similar to his own ideal of life's "wonder" and is approached analogously. The methods of art of both are used in a subversive attack on man's "life excluding" wall of rationality and are mutually directed toward what surrealist spokesman Andre Breton describes boldly as "a general and emphatic *crisis in consciousness*" dedicated to a revelation of the "marvellous." Nahma Sandrow's excellent study *Surrealism: Theatre, Arts, Ideas* reveals further surrealist characteristics which may be compared with Patchen's. Both believe in purging violence by expressing it; anger and joy are their predominant moods; both draw on the subconscious for imagery, often engaging in automatic writing; both mix abstract and concrete in their attempt to reconcile seeming opposites: sublime and trivial, universal and individual, sacred and profane. Both include the use of associative and rationally incongruent structure, as well as the characteristic use of titles for separate and ironic comment. But a fundamental and the paramount affinity is their shared ideal of the master creator of life and art — the "total artist."

Sandrow suggests how centrally important the conception of the artist was to the Surrealists: "They were artists ... primarily because art was for them a means of living the surrealist life with intense awareness. In fact, the surrealist felt ... that one's self is his primary artistic creation and must be fully achieved."[25] Thus for the surrealist not only is art his life, but his life is art. Sandrow adds: "Certainly Dada and surrealism both were considered by their members to be primarily philosophies and ways of life rather than schools of art."[26] Not only does this phenomenon indicate a breakdown in the conventional distinctions between life and art, it also reveals the ideal of the artist totally engaged in his art. Certainly all artists are engaged in their art, but for Patchen and the Surrealists this involvement is carried to an extraordinary degree. Both rebel with anti-art in order to establish new committed approaches to art, to break down the old life and art distinctions. "Let the poet be one with his own life,"[27] is Patchen's requirement. In short, this new conception of the "total artist" manifests itself in both Patchen and the Surrealists in at least four ways: 1) life and art become inseparable, 2) the master artist ignores all distinctions among artistic genres, 3) the artist becomes a "performer" of his art, and 4) there is an effort to redefine the role of artist and audience as the audience is pulled into the life of creating art.

James Boyer May, among others, as an editor and personal friend of Patchen has commented on the close identification of Patchen's life and art: "His personal being and doings concur with what his writings are and advocate. For while as a man he is much besides, the poet *is* Patchen."[28] Later May comments even more directly, "He is as he writes."[29] Besides the engaged relationship of his life and art, Patchen fits well the conception of the master artist. He defines himself loosely as a "writer," as one who performs in multimedia within a single work: "Poetry is writing. Maybe what I am talking about is not poetry (the stuff the critics are yammering about). In whose name is the criterion? Dante's I think. Homer's, I think. Dostoevski's, I think. They were writers, and they wrote. I am a writer, and I shall write. The term 'poet' is a convenience of the middle-class. I declare myself a writer. I want room to move around."[30] This declaration, made early in his career, underlies all of the art he was to create, as poetry and prose, jazz, and painting are blended by this total artist.

Asserting his belief in an art form to embrace all media at once, Patchen explained to Henry Miller, "I think that if I ever got near an assured income I'd write books along the order of great canvases, including everything in them — huge symphonies that would handle poetry and prose as they present themselves from day to day and from one aspect of my life and interests to another."[31] Patchen also attempts to fulfill the surrealist demand to perform his art upon his audience. His poetry-and-jazz readings (to be explored in a treatment of his poetry-jazz form) throughout the United States and Canada in the late 1950's are legendary and were complemented by television performances and by excellent recordings. His picture-poems come as close as Patchen could, under the physical limitations of his spinal injury, to a performed art acting upon the viewer.

The final manifestation of the "total artist" as one who attempts to redefine a closer relationship between art, artist, and audience fits Patchen well. Of the surrealists Sandrow indicates, "We see that the thrust of every surrealist art work is toward personal union. And for this union to occur, the artist himself had to be in a position to participate."[32] Under this concept of a "personalism" of style, Patchen is understood as one who seeks to deeply engage his audience and himself — through art — to life.

CHAPTER 5

An Art of Wonder

"I cannot conceive of any way in which I could lose the sense of wonder. To me that would be death."[1] While attributing death to the loss of wonder, Patchen also is identifying wonder as the essence of life, the life his art would engage us in. As joint positive requirements of his vision, "engagement" and "wonder" are fused under the concept of the unity of life. One ultimately becomes engaged in "wonder." As models for this ideal Patchen suggests Blake and Shakespeare. He concludes an interview with praise for "what Blake felt — the universal in the grain of sand, all humanity in one person. And that one person being all people. . . . Shakespeare shows in his plays that this is true, that all people are one person, and they all are all understood, they are all."[2] Patchen, too, seeks an engagement in this *all,* and it is to come through feeling and love as well as through the free, open, and imaginative spirit of wonder.

More than an inflated description,[3] "wonder" emerges as Patchen's ideal reality located within man's capacity for true self-realization. He laments its present loss — "Men have destroyed the roads of wonder. / And their cities squat like black toads / In the orchards of life" (*C.P.* 322) — and his true design is to regain it. His art is dedicated to inviting man along and instructing him on the ideal path of "wonder." His writing, therefore, defines, describes, and demonstrates "wonder." Dismissed by many critics as mere lofty rhetoric, it is actually an ideal concept in the Romantic tradition of Rousseau, Wordsworth, Coleridge, Emerson, Thoreau, and Whitman — men who, refusing to *analyze* away existence, sought instead to *behold* the universe and its underlying unity. Recent critics, Raymond J. Nelson, James Schevill, and Richard Hack, have acknowledged wonder as central to Patchen's vision. Hack proclaims "the richness of Patchen's personal uni-

70

verse: he was energetic and open enough to plunge and soar in the larger psychic life that most individuals are too unaware of or too afraid to unlock, even in times of crisis."[4] As an ultimate means of expanding man's consciousness, the concept of "wonder" shapes Patchen's vision of life and the functional form of his art.

Wonder is for Patchen an ideal state of existence as well as man's way of arriving at himself, his true life essence. It thus becomes the 'process' — object and action — of man's self-actualization from within. In addition to its Romantic and transcendental roots, "wonder" as a means of knowing the universe from within is also characteristic of the aforementioned surrealism with its "inner model" and of Eastern philosophy, epitomized in the example of Herman Hesse's *Siddhartha.* We therefore find Patchen exclaiming in his love poems, "I am come to her wonder / Like a boy finding a star in a haymow" (*C.P.* 171), where wonder is presented as her state and his approach to it. In a later poem he declares, "The world is not very big / There is only room for our wonder" (*C.P.* 180) where it becomes the shared state of their engagement. *Poemscapes,* a collection of humorous and fabulous prose poems, is full of the world's wonder images and concludes with the simple and final life instruction to "Wonder it!"[5] One thus approaches and finds wonder within, in the way man beholds the universe. Another key to Patchen's perspective on wonder is provided in his explanation of the active and unifying flow which underlies existence: "All appearances have a common origin in the unseeable fluidity *which issues forth from the action of its flowing.* Existence is verb."[6] The ideal existence is wonder. Thus Patchen's theory of man's divinity, the unity of life, and a necessary engagement are all embodied in his concept of wonder — man's true state of being.

I *The Model of Wonder*

Children are seen as Patchen's models of wonder, and what he admires in them helps to define his belief. Freedom, spontaneity, innocent questioning, and an acceptance of the validity of the imagination are the ideal qualities he finds in the child. Patchen again reveals his affinity with Blake, Wordsworth, Emerson, and Whitman, and with contemporaries Robert Duncan, E. E. Cummings, and Lawrence Ferlinghetti. When he shouts to us to "BE AS CHILDREN AGAIN!" (*Sleepers,* 87) we should be alerted, how-

ever, that Patchen urges us to embrace the ideals found in childhood and not an idealized view of childhood. Like Blake's *Songs of
Innocence and Experience,* Patchen's celebration of childhood is
conditioned by an awareness of the imminent and tragic loss of
wonder that ensues the child's "development." His introduction to
Blake's *The Book of Job* reveals his understanding of Blake as well
as their shared views. Patchen's paraphrase discloses his own view
of wonder as much as Blake's:

> Do what you want and what you want will make
> everybody more beautiful.
> Each thing that truly lives is sanctified.
> You speak of self-restraint. Should the sun?
>
> The only thing which should be suppressed is
> suppression; should be killed is killing; should
> be restrained denied retarded is restraint denial
> etc., etc. [7]

These declarations of spontaneity and freedom of response are followed by an affirmation of the imagination:

> The only thing which can live is life. And
> death, naturally, has nothing to do with dying.
> The material world exists because *somebody*
> went to the bother of imagining it.
> Each really *new* one can do it better than the
> last.
>
> All the Great are unborn! [8]

Life is sanctified; restraint is death; the imagination holds the key
— these are the ideals found in childhood.

"I have a theory ... There's a good deal of us in what we
imagine" (*Memoirs,* 37) states the narrator of Patchen's *Memoirs.*
And in *Albion Moonlight* Patchen further proclaims the life of the
imagination, "There are worlds in our heads whose beauty is
beyond our understanding" (*Albion,* 112). Recognizing the validity
and the reality of the imagination is the first step toward wonder. In
"Delighted with Bluepink," one of his many invitations to wonder,
Patchen reveals how the delights of this world are inclusive of the
imagination:

> Flowers! My friend, be delighted with what you like,
>   but with *something*.
> Be delighted with something. Yesterday for me it was
>   watching
> sun on stones; wet stones. . . .
>
> But today what delights me is thinking of bluepink flowers!
> Not that I've seen any . . .
> Actually there isn't a flower of any kind in the house —
>   except in my head. (*C.P.* 441)

The "bluepink flowers" of the imagination are no less real in Patchen's cosmology than the delights of the sun and stones. In childlike wonderment the boundaries of reality and consciousness are expanded, and from Patchen's own marvelous imagination a whole world of fantastic fables, creatures, and other imaginings spring. He finds in the imagination an affirmation of the wonder, as he leads his readers along the "creature-steeped way of ease for man in the unchartable and awesome continents of himself" (*C.P.* 481).

Coupled with this belief in the imaginative validity of each man's mind is a celebration of the miracles of daily living. It too is a quality Patchen finds exemplified most strikingly in children, as he declares in "This Summer Day":

> O all Life must be this crowd of kids
> watching a hummingbird fly around itself. . . .
>
> This sudden beautiful *excitement*
> O have ye buckets great enough
> to catch so much Wonder in! (*C.P.* 325)

Patchen sees life's unity and man's divinity affirmed in the child's open response to the universe where he beholds "a sense of wonder, a sense of identification with everything that lived, with everything that had its being around him."[9] His art insists that all men "recognize the inescapable poignancy of the world, and all that takes place in it."[10] An analogy with Walt Whitman is valid and revealing, for it is Whitman's belief in "Miracles" that confirms their shared vision: "Why, who makes much of miracles? / As to me I know of nothing else but miracles."[11] Again in "Song of Myself" Whitman testifies to the wonderwork of daily life:

> I believe a leaf of grass is no less than the journey-work
>   of the stars,
> And the pismire is equally perfect, and a grain of sand,
>   and the egg of the wren, . . .
>
> And a mouse is miracle enough to stagger sextillions of
>   infidels.[12]

Patchen gives this Romantic theme contemporary relevance when he too uses the mouse as an argument with science for the miracles of living:

> & so the little fieldmouse said:
> "All right, but first explain
> something easy —
> Like, for instance,
> Why does my heart beat?
> Otherwise, you'll never convince anyone
> That blowing up the world
> Shows how far-along smart you've got —
>   It'll just plain, simple
> Prove how crazy you are!"[13]

Wonder, here expressed in the heartbeat of a mouse, is always held against the analytical and rationalizing madness of man.

In his poem "WONDER REMAINS WONDER" Patchen attempts a definition expressed in wonder's own images: "There is in each life a quality, a special fragrance of the bone and of the flesh, individual, unmistakable, exactly as it issued from the spirit's mold. A quality which nothing can in any manner alter."[14] Elsewhere this transcending spiritual quality is explained in terms of an *animal essence.* Such a recognition of the essential spiritual reference for animal life largely explains the creature and animal imagery that pervades Patchen's writing and drawing. "You know that trees are animals like any other; just as flowers and lakes — and even what we think and what we say, what we dream, what we imagine — these too are animals, animals like any others."[15] Affirming the spiritual essence of all life, Patchen's explanatory *Because It Is* further declares:

> For existence
> Is an animal substance, indivisible, and hence, unknowable;
> And all things — stars, brides, and apple boughs —
> And non-things, too — such as "history's happenings" —
> Are but its cells and bones and tissues.[16]

Such a spiritual force, which Emerson expressed as the Over-Soul uniting all life, Patchen terms an animal essence. For both men it was the wonder to behold in life.

Patchen, like poets Blake, Wordsworth, Cummings, and Duncan, looks at the change from childhood to adulthood and sees a tragic loss of wonder. The process of an education to this world of madness means not only the loss of innocence but of man's ability to marvel. "I say the thread breaks, that the man does not come out of the child — God knows where the man comes from or where the child goes ... and as for growing up, most men grow down ... there is not an ounce of sense in any of it" (*Albion,* 151). To Cummings the essential loss of childhood can be summarized as "down they forgot as up they grew,"[17] and the present education into adulthood is depicted as "all ignorance tobaggins into know / and trudges up to ignorance again."[18] To Patchen this desire to "know" the world through analysis alone is something imposed by adults and is representative of a death to wonder. He explains in "O What a Revolution!": "Children don't want 'to know,' they want to increase their enjoyment of not knowing. But people will go on Thursdaying on Wednesdays" (*C.P.* 448). Patchen's friend Robert Duncan has written on this shared view of the crippling of human consciousness by an imposed education: "Parental love goes only as the child goes along with the parent. This is the crippling of the imagination or rather its starvation. The world of wonders is limited at last to the parent's will."[19]

The call is for rebirth. Life should not be a pattern of 'development' into an adult state but a process of continual rebirth into the miracles of existing. Patchen joins a line of venerated poet-pipers who call to the child in man to be reborn in wonder. There is Blake who beckons to man in "The Voice of the Ancient Bard": "Youth of delight, come hither, / And see the opening morn, / Image of the truth new-born."[20] Following Rosseau and Wordsworth, Cummings declares that "We can never be born enough,"[21] and Ferlinghetti expresses their shared design: "I am waiting / perpetually and forever / a renaissance of wonder."[22] The Patchen call for rebirth can only be realized through recognizing the model of childhood ideals — where imagination is real, where life is a daily miracle, and where man is free to respond in wonder to his world. His "Continuation of the Landscape" speaks of such a world:

> Only through losing your place
> in this overlapping circle of wombs,
> can we attain to that ultimate pattern
> Where childhood selects its running wing and grave.
> (*C.P.* 210)

Far from an escape into fantasy, wonder is presented as Patchen's truest form of "being." The "ultimate pattern" of life for Patchen is that set by a free, imaginative, and continual creation of the world. One therefore expects and finds in his art, methods of creating in wonder.

II   *The Creation of Wonder*

Though most of Patchen's comments on the act of creating appear within his works, Norman Thomas records the advice Patchen gave to him on writing: "Remember that you were probably more creative when you wrote the words than when, later, you go over the page proofs.... Never be afraid to show what you feel.... Being foolish isn't the worst thing."[23] Feeling, impulse, and whim seem to be guiding principles of creation and of wonder. Patchen has always been a model of the artist who dares, who risks experimental flaws in a pursuit of involved creation.

In a poem revealing his method of creating in wonder, Patchen speaks of his intuitive theory. It is titled revealingly: "If a Poem Can Be Headed into Its Proper Current / Someone Will Take It within His Heart / to the Power and Beauty of Everybody." Suggested here are both a requisite trust in one's creative act and by "Proper Current" an alliance with projective verse which seeks to become a medium or "field" for an expression of the authentic forces of life. Like Charles Olson and Robert Creeley, Patchen identifies a source of creation in the felt pulse:

> And the music of the silence flows on the world
> With a rhythm and a pulse which are changed
> In the blood-beat as the heart's course by death
>
> And hearing is heard as in the very sea. (*C.P.* 389)

Embodying the intuitive method which he prescribes "For the common good / Of the one creature which everything is" (*C.P.* 390), this poem presents an image of the poet as a creator who is "bound and swayed as we are by the blood's orchestration / Bound and swayed as we are by the orchestration within us" (*C.P.* 391). Written in 1949 before Olson would arrive at similar theories in "Projective Verse," this poem is preceded by an earlier one, "Poems Which Are Written by the Soul" (1945), which also deals with the subject of creativity. Asserting the ultimate unexplainability of the true poem, he further defines the source of creation:

> The meaning of the image is always clear;
> But what the Thing is we may only sully.
>
> Where the particular and the universal
> The infinite and the minute, join,
> Is the province of the soul —
> Here the red deer carries continents on its back,
> And the towns of God lift their real and pure spires.
> > > (*C.P.* 327)

This is an excellent description of Patchen's best poetry, which contains the necessary and inexplicable combination of "the particular and the universal / The infinite and the minute." In this land of the soul, Patchen's wonder assumes form, as he demonstrates in the mixture of the particular "red deer" and the infinite "continents" or in the combined image of "the towns of God."

Through this startling blend of infinite and minute images Patchen creates a sense of wonder in his art and his audience. Later, in one of the picture-poems from *Hallelujah Anyway,* he suggests to artists who would be wonder-makers: "O there's no point saying anything except what you can't / Take your hand and lead yourself into the unneeding place-of-you."[24] This creative theory lends credence to Patchen's mystical aspects, but, more than that, it suggests wonder as both an effect and a means of his art. He seeks to create *through* wonder as a demonstration of its own authenticity. The

Patchen world of the imagination is affirmed by the art he derives
from it.

Two poems which indicate the importance of wonder in
Patchen's later art are "In Shadings of an Obscure Punishment"
and "Folly of Clowns." The former begins with Patchen's statement of his shifted concern from social to personal salvation:

> It is strange that only now as the world dies
> Do I fill with the blood of my special creature.
> I have no neighbor, for I come in a wrong time —
> And everything is wounded that I would make clean. . . .
>
> Therefore I shall forfeit nothing
> If I deal with the wondrous lights
> That are beginning to sparkle
> Somewhere on an unseen continent. (*C.P.* 255)

Recognizing his "special creature" ability to restore man through
creating in the "unseen continents" of wonder, Patchen's direction
is clear. His animal and creature fables, his irrational verse, his
poetry-and-jazz experiments, and his painting and poem forms all
emerge from the mid 1950's to 1972 in what may be termed the culminating "wonder period" of his art. Turning to the "Folly of
Clowns," he reveals how a personal engagement in life's wonder
can answer to the madness. He invites us to:

> Come laughing when the wind
> Has blown a hole
> In the world. . .
>
> O come here laughing anyway
> And let your head
> Be daft
> With sun and glitter of
> Running
> Naked beside the waters. (*C.P.* 410)

One turns from the incessant insanity to the freedom of the miraculous. By 1957 his celebration of love had joined that of wonder; as
he declares in "The Rose of Life" the only meaningful message of
life is "A message of Passionate Folly!" (*C.P.* 480). In a mad
world, the "folly" of love and wonder becomes the only approach

open to the poet-prophet of mankind. Thus Patchen's visionary pathway broadens yet remains consistently clear.

Patchen's respect for what true poetry born out of wonder can do is attested in the long poem to the "word" given in *Albion Moonlight*. It explains his functional aesthetics:

> The word is the saying
> The word is the echo of our dreaming
> The word is the web we take from the womb...
>
> The word is the prayer of the unbeliever to his belief...
> The word is the way a child thinks...
>
> The word is the answer to the darkness. (*Albion,* 237–238)

Based on an intuitive and spontaneous vision of life, the *word* for Patchen becomes the *world* he creates through an art of madness, engagement, and wonder. By example as a man and by the model of his artistry, Patchen seeks to forge and mold that art which will complete his vision of life. Principles and goals emerging from his world view thus provide the foundation of his vision of art and in turn of those experimental forms created to unite life and art. Patchen is ever the poet-prophet and "world-crier" who would make a new world through an art designed "not to throw light but be light" (*Sleepers,* 268).

CHAPTER 6

The Prose

G IVEN a vision of an absurd or insane world, the artist finds himself in a void to which he must create a response. He may choose to turn to his art as the only source of meaning and thus burn himself out in some spiritual sacrifice to the muse, an art for art's sake existence. Or he may respond to the world's absurdity through an artistic sensibility that leads him to capture the world in equally absurd forms, absurd art. What separates Patchen's art from the art for art's sake response or that of the Absurdists is that Patchen envisioned an immensely meaningful, even beautiful, world lying just below the smothering blanket of man-made absurdity. Society is insane, and the world is meaningful. This is the horrific and paradoxical vision from which Patchen's art evolves.

And what of the existing art forms? They must bear the attack of an advancing guard of experimentation, for they have ultimately failed. They are humanities which have failed to humanize. The rebellion, therefore, is against them as it is against the other forms of man's gaping insanity and failure. It is from this sense of despair with the traditional forms and conventions of art that Patchen moves to create his own protean barrage of experimental art, as an affront to social insanity and as an affirmation of the world's denied wonder. Apocalyptic in its conception, Patchen's art is simultaneously opposed to the traditional veneration of art and dedicated to a continued affirmation of the world. The experimental forms which he created to fulfill his vision are thus the truest definition of his art.

*   *   *

Out of this rejection of "art" and affirmation of life came experimentation and Patchen's whole gamut of prose forms. While normal genre distinctions cannot contain the radical range of his innovations, loosely applied they can help us grasp the scope of the art he would renew. Though primarily known as a poet, Patchen has written seven prose books and several short prose pieces. His *Albion Moonlight* stands as his greatest single achievement outside of the *Collected Poems*. The variety of his experimental prose is both remarkable and revealing. His poetry, however, is never far from his prose as he works for a synthesis of forms through juxtaposition and blending.

I A Summary of the Prose

"Bury Them in God," the most significant of Patchen's rare experiments with the short story form, juxtaposes a young boy's awakening to life in an industrial small town with the artist's attempts to render that life later in a Greenwich Village flat. Published in the *New Directions 1939* collection, it contains the autobiographical detail and proletarian theme of his early work. Deceptively simple in its opening atmosphere of the milltown proletarian family, the story soon launches into a rite of passage theme as the first person narrator probes his relationship to his family, particularly to his father, during the funeral preparations for the dead sister Noreen. The social and family background are Patchen's own, and the physical detail and psychological depth of the family situation are convincingly rendered in the Lawrencian mode. By the end of the story, however, we are to confront in classic miniature most of Patchen's characteristic experimental prose forms. Fragmentary shifts and flashbacks in plot compel us into the mental and emotional turmoil of the adolescent narrator contending with sexual awakenings, loss of innocence, search for self identity, and love for his dead sister. All are embodied in the youth's struggle to contend with the whirlpool of his own relationships to life.

In the midst of the funeral scene, however, the reader is suddenly yanked into the reality that this is a story being written by a writer in a flat somewhere in New York. Whether this is a flash forward in the boy's own life is never established. Instead we watch a writer compose the story in which we have been engrossed, a characteristic perspective for the Patchen reader. Again and again, most noticeably in *Albion Moonlight,* Patchen uses the emotional distancing and aesthetic proximity of the Quaker's Oats box advertisement or the box in a box in a box situation, that of a story written about a writer writing a story. In this new perspective of watching the art happen from reality, it is the writer's struggle that we share, his groping for an expression of the story's reality. Patchen is actually defying our aesthetic distance from art by admitting that it is art and by engaging us instead in the real struggle to create it. Back in the flat the writer talks with Swanson, another author, about art and the problem of making it from reality. Melville, Heine, Whitman, and Hawthorne are discussed along with the current critical pursuits of Twain and E. A. Robinson.[1]

We are returned to the tale and the funeral scene now with a double sense of watching the story happen for the writer as well as to the characters. By uniting the multiple realities of imagination and creation, Patchen maintains an emotional involvement and an intellectual distance simultaneously. The writer tries an ending of violence. He crawls into bed with his mistress, only to arise and try a compassionate ending. He returns to Mary in bed but awakens again and ends by beginning all over: "I begin to write: It happened fifteen years ago in Ohio. I was a sensitive lad."[2] We end, not with a conclusion, but with a continuation, a favorite device of Patchen's prose, a refusal to tie off the life of the tale and to allow it to stop happening for the reader. Patchen has achieved his triple perspective in form through the reality of the first person narrator, the struggling writer, and the author's own writing of the story. This small classic anti-story engages in the overall struggle of his art, to find meaning and form in existence.

In the 1941 advance advertisement for Patchen's *The Journal of Albion Moonlight* he revealed this much of the book's purpose: "It is a journal of the summer of 1940 — that plague-summer when all the codes and ethics which men had lived by for centuries were subjected to the acid test of general war and universal disillusionment. I have tried to make an imperishable record of that time."[3] This totally experimental work, which aims at capturing man's consciousness of his insane times, contains all the experimental prose forms that Patchen ever developed. It will be examined more closely later on as the model of his anti-novel, the main subject of this chapter.

Memoirs of a Shy Pornographer (1945) which Patchen jestingly called "An Amusement" is a further attempt at experimental fiction. Though it is certainly the most memorable title he ever wrote, it is a lighter work than his *Albion Moonlight* or *Sleepers Awake* and falls short of their comprehensive intent. However, *Memoirs* does contain many of Patchen's most exciting and characteristic formal innovations and is a direct reflection of his world view. Using the writer-narrator for fictional perspective, Patchen allows Albert Budd (A. Budd) to provide a first person narration of the absurd times as he and the lame Priscilla stand in contrast with a corrupted society by their ideal quest for love and faith. Innocent and gullible, like Melville's Billy Budd and a perfect twin of Voltaire's Candide, Albert Budd stumbles through a series of misadventures with contemporary society, enabling Patchen to mirror the social madness through its own popular culture of literature, music, drugs, and crime. Kenneth Rexroth sees Patchen's satiric method as one of creating modern anti-heroes "reduced to their simplest elements and then filtered through the screen of the commodity culture. Lancelot becomes the Thin Man, Ulysses is worked over by Mickey Spillane, the Poet is confused with Flash Gordon, love scenes slip in and out in the idiom of Ranch Romances, Tristan and Iseult are played by Elvis Presley and Kim Novak."[4] The ability to create caricatures is one of Patchen's achievements in this strange mixture of detective story parody, surrealistic dream narration, love story, and protest. One encounters detectives, drug addicts and pushers, motion picture stars, literary critics, politicians, jazzmen, and writers in this bizarre circle of people and events. Discontinuity of event is used to capture the absurd feel of contemporary society. Rexroth's analysis of form and function relationships is entirely accurate: "The idiom of science fiction or the blood-on-the-scanties school of detective stories accurately but naively reflects the mass psychosis, however skillfully it may be rigged to augment that psychosis and sell commodities."[5] Using this form of writing against itself, Patchen makes his own societal mirror out of the scraps of society he finds in the streets. Yet behind it all is the growing awareness which Patchen presses upon us that "Wars and the plague-sores left by wars shall not be ended until mankind turns from the murder *which is practiced every day by everyone*" (*Memoirs,* 176). It is the daily madness we inflict upon each other which results in these grotesque extremes of society's absurd.

Three of Patchen's experimental prose books were published in 1946: *Sleepers Awake, They Keep Riding Down All the Time,* and

Panels for the Walls of Heaven.[6] He also published his revealing "A Letter to God" that same year in Henry Miller's *Patchen: Man of Anger and Light* with their shared publisher, Padell.

"A Letter to God" as the title indicates, is Patchen's attempt to deal directly with God, talking, arguing, pleading, and challenging Him in direct confrontation. It contains autobiographical detail as well as Patchen's struggle with his theology. The epistolary form is revealing and characteristic of Patchen's prose, where poetry and prose blend in a personal statement of belief. Not primarily fiction, though full of imaginative response, it uses direct statements, fragmentary structure, and contains some poetry. The real key to this brief work is in the dated entries indicative of a journal, and like a journal its directness needs little interpretation. As pages from 'The Journal of Kenneth Patchen' it communicates authenticity and the writer's own conclusions:

> That the things of labor belong to all men.
> That the things of spirit live in all men.
> That the things of God are on earth for the use of all men.
>
> None shall kill when all are completed.
> None shall hate when all are at love.
>
>   August, 1943.[8]

This accurate and concise paraphrase of Patchen's positive vision includes the elements of love, engagement, brotherhood, and wonder in a cosmic recognition of the unity of all life.

They Keep Riding Down All the Time is a short fictional work dealing with the personal and universal problem of creating in a world gone mad. Again the first person narration of a writer struggling to write draws the reader into an engaged experience of reality through the reflective commentary and experiencing consciousness of a sensitive artist. In a characteristic intimate and direct attack on the reader's sensibilities, Patchen's narrator communicates the fatalistic feel of the downward riding of life while simultaneously revealing the only alternatives of love, humor, and creation. Concluding that "The only art form that's worth a damn is when a man tries to offer up something out of himself, out of his own head, his own emotions, his own dreams, his own heart, his own guts,"[9] Patchen presents an image of his own art. The compassion and protest are embodied in his cry: "O let the rain and the snow and the bitter wind beat in vain on the shacks of the poor and keep that beautiful goddam horn blaring away right in the face of all their filthy governments."[10] Content, character, and form are those of art struggling to *be,* as Patchen's own "horn" blares into the night.

Panels for the Walls of Heaven was described by Patchen as "poems-in-prose," and he was to later rewrite them for the 1968 *Collected Poems* giving them more poetic form and revising some of the thematic content, in most cases softening his anger and pessimism during the 1940's. In their original state, these works have a separateness of form like individual poems yet a composite effect like prose chapters as they are both associated by theme and enveloped in the artist's stance toward reality. Like *Sleepers Awake* of that year, *Panels for the Walls of Heaven* contains much diversity — concrete poems, picture-poems, drawings, and brief prose pieces of love and terror. It has no overall story line, but is, rather, a kinetic composite of fragmentary pieces united by world vision and artistic conception.

Sleepers Awake is probably what William Faulkner would term as Patchen's most "magnificent failure." Magnificent in its Herculean attempt to include all of life, failure (as all books must be) in its inability to capture life's comprehensive splendour. This work, which attempts to make that great canvas of a book to include everything, is Patchen's *Finnegan's Wake.* It is his longest, most experimental, language centered, and most incomprehensible prose writing. A book of extreme engagement and wonder, it defies paraphrase and can only be described. All genres are mixed in its anti-novel form containing little plot, yet excellent sections of concrete poetry, early examples of drawings, typographical explosions, central Patchen themes on life and art, as well as a fictional narrative framework to almost contain it all. The problem is that this framework does not contain it all; the reader is exposed to and is expected to do too much. Patchen would have the reader make his own book, one assumes, but the fragmentary givens are at once too loose and too restrictive. In his attempt to create the loosest structure possible, Patchen has also imposed his own private views and definite themes to contend with. It should be noted that the Surrealists suffer similar problems in writing a long sustained work based so crucially on impulsively imaginative and illogically juxtaposed structure. Witness that there are few attempts and no truly successful surrealist novels.

Although *Sleepers Awake* does not succeed for the present day
readers, it does contain some of Patchen's most brilliant prose seg-
ments as well as the bulk of his concrete poetry. One justification
lying behind such a radical and risky experiment in form is given by
the first person narrator who explains the functional form: "Slam
the feeling in. Anything get in your way, knock it down! Hold the
pen with both hands if you have to. Make the whole wonderful big
damn thing go bulling up and shake the living daylights out of
them!" (*Sleepers*, 292). Patchen would scream us awake from the
precipice with his methods, justified by the desperation of the times
and the ready and impinging beauty of the life we are sleeping
through. He states frankly, "if the artist loses now this world is
doomed and I think the human imagination is being murdered"
(*Sleepers*, 373). His form demands our active and sympathetic
imagination. A second theory behind the form lies in Patchen's
belief that the old forms were too restrictive for life:

> It is time that books be allowed to
> OPEN INTO THE UNKNOWN —
>   "What, sir, does that mean?"
> — books must be allowed to get out of hand, to wander
> off on their own account —   (*Sleepers*, 86)

The book thus includes illogical associative structure, an ironic
anti-hero in Aloysious Best, omission, fantasy, as well as a whole
bag of typographical tricks all encompassed in the loose and inclusive form of a wonder book. Very much like Federico Fellini's film
8½, the search involved in the act of creation becomes the cohering
plot structure. Ultimately the main theme as well as the main relationship between author and reader is one of trust and belief. We
must trust in the author as he instructs us in the demands of his art
and world view. However, his bombastic cursing and screaming at
the reader is overdone and fails here to demonstrate the compassionate wholeness of his life vision.

The segmented structure of this book is further reinforced by the
1972 publication of "Angel Carver Blues" explained as "a section
from an early version of *Sleepers Awake*,"[11] and by the book's
inclusion of the earlier publication "Every Time a Door Is Opened
Somebody's Heart Gets Busted." Perhaps the reason Patchen lists
"Bury Them in God" as his only short story is because all his

subsequent shorter prose pieces found their way into the open format of such anti-novels as *Sleepers Awake* which offered the background of a common view of life and art.

See You in the Morning, Patchen's only conventional novel, appeared in 1947, a year after he had written in "A Letter to God" that "I have no children because I couldn't feed them. My wife never has a new coat and I may have to write novels."[12] *See You in the Morning* is a potboiler catered to popular tastes which first appeared condensed in *Ladies' Home Companion* magazine with tentative plans for Sears Roebuck distribution. Though it sharply conflicts with his view of art, the content does not violate his philosophy of life. As a subtitle indicates, it is "A Novel of Love and Faith,"[13] the story of a young couple who fall in love at a summer resort despite the imminence of death. The only formal experimentation is the adoption of an omniscient yet first person narrator, suggestive of a guarding angel. Patchen fails at this mercenary form of fiction — melodramatic plot and sentimental dialogue — though he may have paid a few bills with it.

Fables and Other Little Tales was written in 1950 and appeared first as *Jargon #6* in 1953. It has been reprinted subsequently with the addition of Patchen drawings as *Aflame and Afun of Walking Faces.*[14] It is a book indicative of the later Patchen, full of fun and play, with dips into the irrational source to create a collection of short tales and fables that inspire imaginative states of mind akin to wonder. Patchen creates an oral feel to the narrations (he later released a recording of his reading them) and engages in characteristic antics of word play, elaborate puns, ironic juxtapositions, and incongruous structure. As the first of his works during the Wonder Period, it will be considered further in Chapter ten as a model of Patchen's irrational tales and verse.

The last of his prose books appeared in 1958, though he continued to write some prose fragments for the picture-poems. *Poemscapes* (1958) is more accurately designated as prose poems, and it will be examined as such later on. The "poemscapes" are brief (often a sentence or two) statements of protest and love directed at life and the reader. Impressionism, surrealism, and imagism combine in the quasi-philosophical statements meant to instruct us in the social madness and to suggest the way to wonder. Worthy of note in *Poemscapes* and in the earlier 1954 *The Famous*

Boating Party is Patchen's distinctly American innovation of humor to the international prose poem form.

More radical than his experiments in poetry, Patchen's experimental prose more openly demonstrates his views on life and art. In them he dares far more, including direct statement. *Albion Moonlight* thus serves as an excellent avenue toward arriving at an understanding of Patchen.

II   The Journal of Albion Moonlight *as Anti-Novel*

If Ezra Pound's premise is correct, that all true art must "MAKE IT NEW,"[15] then every really new novel is, in a sense, an anti-novel. It must sweep away old conventions and definitions to establish new art. As Philip Stevick points out, this new art must "seduce us into experiencing it in ways which our experience of traditional art has not prepared us for."[16] A ready challenge to the artist to make new forms is always a part of the business of art. What we call avant-garde is merely a designation for those artists who have set out to push beyond established borders of form into new areas of creativity and awareness. Rather than a reaction against the novel, or fiction, or art, the anti-novel is a reaction against the infringement of a restrictive definition of form sanctioned by tradition. Experimentation is at once the artist's cry for life and a demonstration that such life exists. The avant-garde perspective is wholly Patchen's whether he is crying for art or mankind.

The anti-novel is also a direct result of a changing world view. For art to survive, it must keep pace with fundamental changes in man's sense of life; it must have relevance beyond itself as form. The contemporary realization of the absurd, whether it be societal or of human existence itself, demands radically new forms to capture it. Stevick explains, "No one can say, before the fact, what an absurdist fiction ought to look like. The only obligation one can be sure of is the obligation of the writer to experiment, since the one thing a writer who confronts the absurd cannot rely upon is traditional artistic conventions."[17] Patchen's profound sense of the absurd is his acute awareness of the societal insanity which man has made, and it leads to, even demands, a radical new form — the anti-novel.

We realize then that to define an anti-novel is a contradiction in terms, since it is an ever changing form and founded on personal vision. We can, however, define loosely the characteristics of the radically new novel form of this absurdist generation. Stevick's revealing study in *Anti-Story* attempts to define it negatively, by how it reacts and what it reacts against. Thus we find general 'anti' characteristics: "Against Mimesis, Against Reality, Against Subject, Against the Middle Range of Experience, Against Analysis, Against Meaning."[18] Whereas a negative definition only limits the range of meaning, it does suggest the necessity for dropping the old standards for evaluation of fiction forms. Such things as character credibility, coherence and unity of plot, syntactic clarity are dropped in favor of the new standards of truth and applicability to life. Judging the art by its intended goals, we find the anti or experimental novelist making new demands and giving new rewards. "Doing away with many of the fictional conventions we have all grown used to, the 'new novelists' leave us with a phenomenal world broader than we might have expected, virtuous in its execution, and extraordinarily vital."[19] The moment of truth comes when we realize that it is "vital" for art as well as life.

The Journal of Albion Moonlight belongs here, as a most radically experimental form of new novel. By example it has as much to say about the nature of the anti-novel as it does about the general characteristics of all of Patchen's experimental prose. Rather than abandoning the features of the novel, Patchen seeks through innovation to revise and revive the elements of plot, character, structure, narration, and style — original transformations in form evolving out of his crucial confrontation with the world.

Albion Moonlight, Patchen's "chronicle of the human spirit" (*Albion,* 145), is also a record of his unique theories of form. By using the artist-hero-persona of Albion, Patchen is able to both expound upon and demonstrate his theory of art and writing. We are taken into the confidence of the writer Albion, and we share his struggle to find a form which could capture "the plague of universal madness" (*Albion,* 305). Employing his characteristic narrative perspective of an author writing about an author writing, he shocks our sense of aesthetic distance and creates a close identification between the artist Albion and the author Patchen. Our rapport with a conventional author is immediately violated, throwing us into the identical struggle of the artist, to know the world and to find a formal expression of it. His artist-persona also permits him to directly present his theory of writing and form. So we are informed half way through the book of the correct approach: "I consider it my obligation to offer you a few practical suggestions. In the first place, read all of this journal; and for God's sake, don't fight it. Everything will come out fine; I know a hell of a lot more about what is here than you do" (*Albion,* 142). Such statements by Albion concerning his chronicle are also applicable to Patchen's intended "imperishable record"[20] of the times.

The problem of creating in an insane world emerges as the central concern of this anti-novel, a concern that the reader must actively share, as Albion readily acknowledges, "I said that all I wanted to do was make you believe in what I am saying. This could not have happened without your faith. It could never have happened had we not trusted in each other" (*Albion,* 193). The ambiguous distinction between fictional narrator and implied author is one struggle the engaged reader must make, just as he struggles daily to define the ambiguous distinction between fact and fiction in his life. We are engaged, just as his text is. When he tells us that "this book is reading you" (*Albion,* 202), he alerts us that this is a radically new type of writing, a new kind of art experience. He further confides, "I tell you that the writing of the future will be just this kind of writing — one man trying to tell another man of the events in *his own heart*" (*Albion,* 200). In the guise of Albion Moonlight, Patchen creates a form to instruct on the new kind of writing and to demand an active engagement in the life of that writing. Nothing in *Albion Moonlight* is a "given"; all must be grasped.

In this alive context of the artist striving to express life, Patchen is able to present his original and basic assumptions concerning art. Perhaps in justification, but more for clarification, he explains that "Great art must possess an absolute flaw at its very core; otherwise it would be an abuse of the imperishable frailty of all things that exist.... Art must add to the mystery" (*Albion,* 218). With this truth to the forms of existence as a main criterion of his art, we recognize the dangerous and vital looseness of life which Patchen seeks. Against the cries for a false sense of order, Patchen presents a theory of "a form bigger than you or me or anybody" (*Sleepers,* 269). Within this inclusive life form, "there must be a running over of meaning — a spectacular mis-statement" (*Albion,* 162). Like the Neo-Realism movement in art and film, verisimilitude is the chief

criterion. His form is thus conditioned by the insane shape of existence, where "there never was anything but one story since the
world began. A lousy story. A story of how the whole business
doesn't make sense" (*Sleepers,* 364). Embracing the necessary
"mis-statement" and "absolute flaw," his anti-novel form also
contains the necessity "to keep one's hand in, to enjoy that sense of
proportion which comes from a planned deformity" (*Albion,* 144).
Beneath the madness is theme and design, and the two together —
madness and ignored meaning — give the feel of life. As we realize
by the end of the novel, impulse, intuition, fragmentation, and discontinuity of form are all governed by the covert design and control of the artist's sense of life. A basic premise of the book then is
that we must loose ourselves from the false sense of patterning
which restricts us and acknowledge a truer sense of order beneath
the madness. To this end Patchen assures us, "You will see that any
novel I may write is a thing of danger and simplicity — above all, of
simplicity" (*Albion,* 146). This simultaneous awareness of madness
and of new forms of order underlies Patchen's basic approach to
form and content.

Applying this theory, Patchen attacks the false order implied in
the traditional novel form. Albion thus exclaims against "all the
bucket-thumping paraphernalia of a forty-hand novelist's technique keeping me from what I wanted to say" (*Albion,* 66–67).
Albion's concern for and struggles with the novel form, presented
in parodies of fifteen separate and futile attempts at novel writing
within the book, reveal its limitations. The novel form is always
abandoned by Albion for its interference with direct communication, and Patchen subsequently has Albion declare his form to be a
writing and not a novel: "You are to remember this: this novel is
being written as it happens, not what happened yesterday, or what
will happen tomorrow, but what is happening now, *at this writing.*
At this writing! Do you see? I told you before that I would tell part
of our story in the form of a novel: I did not say that I would write
a novel" (*Albion,* 145). The novel form is lacking in immediacy,
and so Patchen has, through Albion, made his own form — one
that we share in making.

His ultimate conclusion on this type of writing comes in the last
pages of *Albion Moonlight:* "I have told the story of the great
plague-summer; as an artist I could have wished that there had been
more structure and design to it — as a man, that there had been less

of the kind there was" (*Albion,* 305). Ultimately the book has written itself from one man's consciousness of life, and although it
lacks the balanced proportion of traditional art, it does so out of
truth to the author's vision of life. For Patchen the demands of life
always come before those of art. Patchen's anti-novel is his record
of the plague-summer of 1940. "I have traced its origins, defined
its boundaries, shown its course. It was too late to write a book; it
was my duty to write all books. I could not write about a few people; it was my role to write about everyone" (*Albion,* 305). The
book begins and ends with Albion's act of writing, and we realize
with Richard Hack that "there is really only one character in *The
Journal of Albion Moonlight,* but this character is everyone, goes
everywhere, sees, feels, and does practically everything."[21]

The book's central plot as well as its central concern emerges as
the action of creating a form to capture life. William Carlos Williams captures, in part, the sense of the book's creating itself:
"Write and discover. Go, move, waggle your legs in more terrible
jungles than any primitive continent could ever afford, the present
day shambles of the Mind. Tortured as you may be, seek love! Such
is the New Life dimly perceived through the mediaeval horrors of
Patchen's hell. This is the cure he is seeking."[22] Williams' own
masterwork, *Paterson,* follows a similar method and form, differ-
ing as his perception of reality differed from Patchen's. Both seek a
new and broader synthesis for life out of an intuitive sense of truth.
Like another modern masterwork, Ezra Pound's *Cantos,* all of
these works seek to derive radically new forms from the artist's free
and authentic sense of life.

"The journal, whether real or imaginary, must conform to only
one law: it must be at any given moment what the journal-keeper
wants it to be at any given moment.... It was my intention to set
down the story of what happened to myself and to a little group of
my friends — and I soon discovered that what was happening to us
was happening to everyone" (*Albion,* 304–305); so says our central
narrator and confidant Albion Moonlight. Above all, the book is a
journal of a remarkable person, and as such it gains its form primarily from the man himself and from his experience with life.
Patchen began keeping his own diary when he was twelve. Thus
realizing that the journal or diary form was integral to the writer,
Patchen seeks here to write a journal of the modern man. Because
keeping a journal or looking back over its entries has the obvious

advantage of revealing the form of one's life, it presented a life form for Patchen's vision. His criticism of Hart Crane's *Bridge* is based on the poem's lack of association with personal structure: "Hart Crane's *Bridge* failed because he didn't think enough about its structure as it had to do with *his own structure as a man.*"[23] This idea, that form grew out of the man, is perfectly illustrated here as structure and narration directly reflect the world view of Albion Moonlight, and, finally, of Patchen himself.

Philip Stevick has asked whether it is possible "to have a fiction which is coherent on its own terms but so tentative and exploratory that its writer seems never entirely clear what its center is."[24] The answer is yes, for that is precisely the anti-novel form Patchen creates in the joint contending sensibilities of writers Albion and himself. As Stevick later explains, "fiction, clearly, 'makes sense' only insofar as the world of experience makes sense in the mind of the writer."[25] Our narrative point of view is of Albion's perpetual stream of consciousness as he struggles to meet the world and to record it. Though much is happening in the text, we are reminded that it all occurs in the consciousness of our narrator-persona. "You are not forgetting that I am still engaged in telling you how I should have begun this journal" (*Albion,* 144), Albion reminds us halfway through the book.

The struggling narrator Albion goes on to explain the creation of necessary ambiguity and ambivalence in his characterization of the fictitious Albion: "I am moved to confide in you again. This time concerning my central, all-important problem: you see, it was necessary for me to go out of my way entirely in order to write *that which I did not want to write.* To put it simply: I had to *become* a person it would kill me to be" (*Albion,* 144–145). Thus the fictional character that Albion creates of himself incorporates evil and violence, the very things Albion as artist opposes. The writer is indeed killed by becoming his character, just as he has learned to mercilessly kill others and accept their murders. This is the creeping insanity that man becomes enslaved in, and we witness it all, through the fishbowl of Albion's disintegrating ego as a character. This duality of good and evil, superego and id, is early revealed of Albion's character when he confides, "I have spent ten years becoming a saint. It was not easy because always the man I was in got in the way. This man's name is Albion Moonlight.... Murder is the new faith and I am its first saint. I am the will, the word, and the deed" (*Albion,* 37, 39).

In the midst of this bloody confession Albion's alter ego obtrudes in italicized speech. He protests: *"I am Albion Moonlight. I do not know the being that says these things. I fear it. It will destroy me. It is but another trick of our enemies. . . . Its fingers are at my throat. The words come from my pen with a life of their own"* (*Albion,* 38–39). This conflict of man's conscience with a murderous molding spirit of the world is a central one and explains much of the ambiguity and ambivalence of Albion's character. Anais Nin describes it as "the nightmare of the fragmented self. All the voices of the subconscious speaking simultaneously."[26]

Struggle is the essence of this book, and it is embedded in the turmoil of Albion as character and as writer-persona. Williams explains Patchen's treatment of his narrator's mind: "Patchen slams his vivid impressions on the page and lets them go at that. He is investigating the deformities of truth which he perceives about him. Not idly. He is seeking, the book is seeking, if I am correct, a new order among the debris of a mind conditioned by old and persistent wreckage."[27] Patchen thus allows the struggle of his own sensibility to be revealed and spread to his readers through the contending sensibility of his narrator-persona. It is a book whose sense and lack of it are a direct reflection of the author's immediate experience with the world.

Since Patchen favors a struggling consciousness for a central narrator, it is not surprising to find his treatment of characterization equally original and deliberately disturbing. Characters float in and out in a sea of changing identities including Jesus and Hitler. "People expand and shrink to the varying proportions of those in *Alice in Wonderland,* and everyday but — desperately,"[28] explains Williams of Patchen's free form within a compelling design. We are not to expect conventional characters in the context of an insane world, Patchen warns us. He has Albion inform us that we are not to manufacture symbolic interpretations, for "my people have meaning in themselves; why try to lard over that meaning by imagining that they are somebody else? . . . I want that understood: things are what I say they are. If any footnotes are needed, I shall be the one to supply them" (*Albion,* 31). However, the approach of seeing symbolic or allegorical value in the characters is a process that Patchen firmly suggests to the reader; yet he alone will tell the reader (directly) of their suggested symbolism: "I have brought into being people of my own size: Jetter, the careless murderer; Billy Delian, in whose useless heart treachery and betrayal lie; Thomas Honey, the physical man who has no endeavor worthy of his strength; Carol, the woman like any other; Jackeen, the visible body of man's desire on earth; Chrystle, the pure child who is in all of us" (*Albion,* 23).

Later, Patchen adds the direct insights that "Jetter is modern man — the killer demanded by the State" (*Albion,* 30), "Chrystle, I may say now, is the girl Christ" (*Albion,* 53). Keddel later appears in the book as an important character — "fine and strong: an innocent before God" (*Albion,* 106). As readers, we are to treat the characters dually as personalities and as assigned allegorical values. Patchen, through Albion, will control the interpretations. To this cast of characters on their flight-quest-caravan Patchen adds: the angry Hitler, the giggling Jesus, the newly found Lost Amazon, and the elusive Roivas (Savior). Characters step in and out of their abstractions to assume personalities and to enter the novels that Albion would write. Above all, they are part of the imaginative reality of writer Albion, who confides his fear that they might "walk out of the book at any time, leaving me to carry on as best I can" (*Albion,* 146). Through this unconventional treatment of character, Patchen achieves both intellectual distance and emotional involvement in one book. The reader watches a merry-go-round of human figures who occasionally step right off and into his life.

If Patchen transforms narration and characterization, what becomes of plot? It too is transmuted in form in favor of the responsive looseness of structural devices. Within the journal form, a sense of time, movement, and collection of data replace plot design. Raymond J. Nelson attempted a brief summary of the plot in his study, and he suitably assigned it a place in the footnotes.[29] Plot discussion is almost meaningless here, for within the over-structure of the journal form there is a nimble and often ambiguous alternating between the plots of Albion's writings and his successive novels. The reader is not meant to keep, indeed finds it impossible to keep, a clear sense of plot. Other structural devices provide form and cohesion in this labyrinthine design.

A sense of time is suggested through the dated entries of the journal. This technique enables Patchen to follow a loose continuity while also using fragmentation and incoherent event to capture the feeling of contemporaneity. He explains his goal of a spontaneity of experience through the journal form: "I was determined to show you precisely what the world is. I had no intention of writing about it, or at it — by Jesus! — I would be that world! But not all the time. Ah, no. I wanted a book that I could read too. I wanted to make a book that I could read for the first time after I had written it" (*Albion,* 145). The visionary goals of his life and art combine here as he attempts to provide in his writing the living spontaneous feel of modern life. What else but discontinuity and fragmentation within a struggle for meaning could express it?

Besides the book's dated entries, other signposts come too late and are a kind of parody of the artificial guides found in conventional novels. Listed under various titles and coming within the last thirty pages of the book are the tables of contents.[30] Comprised of long action descriptions for chapter titles which never appeared, the tables are only obliquely relevant to the journal writing. They do serve at best as a kind of review of the muddle of events in the book. Such internal contents tables also testify to the fact that we are given a middle novel, one with no clear beginning and no definite end. The last statement of the book openly admits: "There is no way to end this book. No way to begin" (*Albion,* 313). This refusal to tie things off, characteristic of Patchen's experimental prose, forces the reader to struggle with the life form of the writing, precisely as he struggles with his own life, using dates as a kind of demarcation for the passing parade of thoughts, feelings, and events.

The journal form also promotes structural coherence through the journey motif. Like a rambling picaresque novel, *Albion Moonlight* compels a vivid sense of movement upon the readers as we follow Albion and his band of characters on their quest to Roivas in the city of Galen. It is, however, a desperate quest that propels the journal forward as they flee the destruction of New York and America chased on by the hungry hounds whose fearful barking echoes throughout the book. Patchen provides a direct address from Albion to explain this necessary sense of movement: "It must be clear to you now, what I am trying to do. With what a sense of shock you must have realized that it is not we who are fleeing from the world: with what joy you exclaimed, 'No, Albion and his friends are not running away — they are speeding to us; we were in

headlong flight, and they have overtaken us—'" (*Albion,* 52).
Caught in this combined sense of flight and quest, we share
Patchen's sense of existence through his journey metaphor and its
correlating motifs. As Anais Nin depicts Patchen's sense of existence, "There are always dogs waiting. They smell death and decay.
There is a recurrent nightmare of martyrdom, persecution, and
punishment."[31]

Patchen's form captures the madness as well as the symbolic
union of those who seek a way out of it all. Later the narrator
admits in tones suggestive of Whitman's, a welcome to all who seek
life: "Dear Camerado! I confess I have urged you onward with me,
and / still urge you, without the least idea of what is our /
destination" (*Albion,* 94). Despite its having no clear destination,
the journey is an essential one. Thus the cohesive device of a quest
for sense does no violence to the aura of incoherence lurking in
Patchen's world. In a later poem from *Hurrah for Anything,*
Patchen captures some of the same sense of movement as the
speaker of "When Is a Stalker Not a Stalker" concludes that he
moves on "Not really knowing whether I'm running from somebody / Or somebody's chasing me because I'm running."[32] It is not
a clear quest with graduating answers, but rather a flight-quest path
designed to capture both the madness and the compulsion to seek
new directions together.

In addition to the fragmented attempts at novels, Albion engages
in parables, impressionistic descriptions of drawings, data collect-
ing devices of lists and notes, speeches, and other fragmentary
writings, some of which may have been lifted directly from his own
notebooks. The parable provides brief jabs at meaning which
parallel the themes and tone of the larger journal form. They are
sprinkled throughout the journal and serve as miniature world
views. One, for example, is of an execution in which the ax falls
and the head rolls onto the platform magically transformed to that
of the executioner (*Albion,* 81) — suggesting both the theme of violence and Patchen's belief in a superior underlying order to existence. A later innovation is Patchen's own variation of the Thematic Apperception Test of psychoanalysts. A drawing is described
(in later works it would be drawn) and the writer registers his
reaction to it:

(Drawing B) I take this to be a little girl modeling

a penis on a snowman.
Thought: Occasionally murderers encase their victims
in snow, even going to the extent of putting on
buttons of coal and inserting clay pipes in the
cold mouths — strange to think of blood seeping out
of a snowman.   (*Albion,* 119)

There are nine of these pieces, each one giving a further look at the
world and its effects on the consciousness of the central narrator.
Patchen uses the psychoanalyst's device to reveal both world insanity and its destructive effects on the mind.

Listing is another favored device for incorporating bits of the
world. The narrator simply breaks off from his story to tell us:

For the sake of the records, I should like to list the following occurrences
— or items, notes, observations, whatever — they may prove of use to
you.

   (1) Jetter has had thirty-seven boils since we set forth. . . .

   (9) We have seen a horned rabbit, a hen's egg having five yolks, a goat
       that spoke French, and a king with a bottom constructed of steel and
       cork. . . .

  (10) Chrystle was murdered and raped by a person or persons unknown (as
       yet). . . .

  (23) I beheld you in a dream. You were singing a song made of blue satin
       and water lilies. (Albion, 129–130)

What is the reader to make of these bits of plot and imaginative
fragments? They constitute another, certainly immediate, means of
conveying information to the reader. They are an authentic part of
the journalist's record keeping.

These journal notes with their loose form and contemporaneous
authenticity take on the form and feel of Patchen's own notes and
jottings on life:

        A short pilgrimage to Herman Mellville's grave. . . .
        That which is not daring is nothing. . . .
        Each day I begin a new life. An endless procession
        of men runs through me. Who am I at this moment?
                                              (*Albion,* 218, 219)

Such brief examples, which run on for pages in the text, suggest random thoughts on life and art, the seeds of larger developments which the reader is left to cultivate. They are held together by the experiencing consciousness of the narrator, the form of the man upon his art. These and other devices, including speeches on capitalism and socialism assigned to characters, all provide the structural replacement for plot. True to his goal of generating a spontaneous life form for his writing, the journal devices create an immediacy of effect which he sought: "Most of this book is written on the air" (*Albion*, 154). Like sky writing, we watch it appear, let it sink in, and then find ourselves moved on to another moment. Patchen is not writing the great American novel; he is writing a work whose immediate objective is to change the consciousness of the reader.

Stylistic devices also help to accomplish the themes and goals of this anti-novel. Primarily, Patchen seeks a simultaneity of effect, as in pages 115–18 where the summoning bold half-inch type message: "I WANT YOU BOYS / TO SHAKE HANDS NOW AND WHEN / THE BELL RINGS COME OUT / FIGHT-ING" is sandwiched between the main narrative flow. This demand of the reader to somehow handle two messages at once is characteristic of Patchen. Pages 253–56 include not two, but three simultaneous messages. One is the important statement on the artist's duty written in poetry; another is an italicized prose confession; and the third is the bold type message of a murderer.[33] The total effect is hard to gauge, but the intent seems to be twofold. First, it is an engaged text, one that demands the reader to actively create the form by how he reads and reacts to the several messages. Secondly, it achieves the incoherent and simultaneous feel of existence where we are continually split between multiple sensory and often contradictory messages, and where we all struggle with our own varied consciousness of life. In another section, a poem on life and the power of the word is interspliced with sections from what Patchen states is "*A Treatise on Field Fortification*, by D. H. Maham" (*Albion*, 235–240). Like dialogue from Theater of the Absurd, Patchen's simultaneous text holds forth the daily contradictions of praise of life and tactics for death. The combination of poetry and prose is also indicative of Patchen's goal of the "total artist," the kind of multimedia master creator necessary for relevant art.

A further characteristic stylistic device of Patchen's experimental prose appears in his treatment of tone and distancing. The style is directly affected by the sense of the central narrative consciousness. Following the example of Whitman's personalism and the surrealists' goal of establishing new and vital relationships between the artist and audience through their art, Patchen seeks to engage us intimately in his perception of the world as well as his act of recording it. As a thinly disguised Patchen, persona Albion makes it clear that "there are two kinds of writers: those who *speak* and those who talk about something" (*Albion,* 304). His position is clarified early in the journal: "My purpose? it is nothing remarkable: I wish to speak to you" (*Albion,* 22). He would engage us in a personal and intimate relationship, and while he, at times, backs us off to an aesthetic or an objective distance from the action of the events, we are never held away from the sustaining action of writing the journal. We are always in and around Albion's head and heart as he struggles to record life. This involved relationship with the writer of the journal is transferred associatively to Patchen's own act of writing.

While it is a relationship of shared concerns, "Our message was this.... WE BELIEVE IN YOU. THERE IS NO DANGER. IT IS NOT GETTING DARK. WE LOVE YOU" (*Albion,* 17), it is also a relationship of deliberate and often upsetting probing. "Do *not* be patient with me — I have a desire to reach beneath the gilt and the ornaments. I leave no room for another word to be said here" (*Albion,* 146), Albion instructs us. Like Whitman's identification of the book with the man, Patchen is writing that book which will be reading us — an engaged and engaging text. His goal is no less than to change us, as he frankly admits, "Some of you will hate my book, for I insist on touching you" (*Albion,* 24). This is where the reader finds himself: pushed and pulled by an intimate relationship in another's life, and, if Patchen's theory is true, in all life. Like close friendship, the demands are as high as the rewards. Within the writings of Albion's journal we have telescopic relationships with the characters and events. We watch most of the characters murder or be murdered; we witness them in acts of intimate and rapacious sex; we struggle with them to their unknown destination. At times we are appalled, at times compassionate, but always it is a deep emotional experience. Patchen has created a self-conscious narrative form to allow and demand such involvement — such change.

A basic shift in tone occurs between the fictive act of writing and the direct statement of Albion to the reader. He self-consciously shifts: "I am tired of writing on the air. I want to say something that will help you. We are animals together.... I have held the body of a dying child in my arms.... We resent our human condition. Death is our color and our smell" (*Albion,* 128). Interpreting the moonlight as a symbol of mad lucidity, William Carlos Williams explains such direct statement as Patchen's necessarily seeking "to reveal his meaning by truthful statement — under conditions of white moonlight. From that to reorder the universe."[34] This bold directness is the overriding feel of the narration, that through complete honesty to self, like the brutally frank narrator of Dostoevsky's *Notes from Underground* who struggles for truth, that through this new sincerity will come change. It requires an open form such as the inclusive journal form, for as Williams explains, "It is, in fact, one mind, his tortured own, that Patchen is travelling through and attempting to reveal to us by its observed attributes. In treating of that there can be no deleting, no pruning no matter how the initiative may wander."[35] Through Albion, Patchen seeks a form that will be both the writer and the writing, and that will thus force an engaged response to the life it recorded.

In *The Journal of Albion Moonlight* Patchen achieves a form totally committed to transforming life. Rejecting the conventional treatments of narration, characterization, plot, style, and distancing, he creates his own forms to capture the world's madness and to engage us in the essential struggle for meaning and new order. He summarizes his own goals: "I believe that the revolutions of the future will be concerned with altering the minds of men, with vomiting out all that is insane for his animal" (*Albion,* 299). He seeks in this original anti-novel form a radical cure that will engage us in an empathetic purging of the world's madness. *Albion Moonlight,* like the many anti-novel and prose experiments to come, was Patchen's most revealing and noble attempt at creating a form to achieve an internal world revolution.

CHAPTER 7

The Poetry-Prose

CHARACTERISTIC of Patchen's belief in the "total artist," his art does not acknowledge artificial genre distinctions. Rather, it is a record of multimedia experimentation urged on by the needs of the times. In addition to the syntheses of jazz and painting with poetry, Patchen broke down the fundamental distinction between poetry and prose. At least six of his books experiment with varying blends of poetry and prose, each designed to give the artist more freedom and efficiency in presenting the world with a living image of itself. There is, in fact, a progressive development to this experimentation beginning with juxtaposition, then to simultaneity of effect, and advancing from crude formal mixtures culminating in the modern synthesis of the prose poem.

I *Juxtaposition*

In *First Will and Testament,* his second book of poetry, Patchen creates a juxtaposed prose poetry form used for most of the work in that volume. Long prose introductions, often exceeding twenty lines, precede the poems themselves. The first prose sentence provides the title, and the remaining portion printed in italics offers supplement or comment (ironic or reinforcing) on the theme of the poem. Many of the prose pieces are borrowings from other works, and they establish their own tone and perspective out of which the poem emerges, as in the following:

> AVARICE AND AMBITION ONLY WERE THE
> FIRST BUILDERS OF TOWNS AND FOUNDERS
> OF EMPIRE; *They said, go to, let us build us a city
> and a tower whose top may reach unto heaven, and
> let us make us a name, lest we be scattered abroad*

102

> *upon the face of the whole earth (Genesis XI:4).*
> *What was the beginning of this city? What was it*
> *but a concourse of thieves, and a sanctuary of criminals?...*
> *Not unlike this was the beginning even of the first*
> *town in the world, and such is the original sin of*
> *most cities: .... To spread our disease. (C.P. 53-5)*

Having established a theme of the corruption of cities, and having given it the historical resonance of Old Testament precedence, the poem launches out in contemporary speech and detail projecting the ancient rhetoric and vocabulary of the prose piece into contemporary myth:

> They scatter me from church to gutter.
> They smear their doings over my hands.
> I am lifted out of wombs
> And never put back anywhere...
> I look up from the grass and down from the cathedral.
> They honor me with the stuff of dogs. (*C.P.* 54)

Through the persona of the perennial and archetypal citizen who becomes an agent of the "disease" of modern insanity Patchen has gained a platform from which to exclaim his proletarian protest and affirmation:

> *I should like to pray now if I can stay out of*
> *a trench to do it*
> There is no war between us, brothers.
> There is only one war anywhere. (*C.P.* 55)

This opening poem of *First Will and Testament* demonstrates Patchen's experimental search for an aesthetic and rhetorical technique through which he might engage and instruct in his world vision. Using selected juxtaposition as a formal device he attempts to engage his readers in the active, creative process of analysis and synthesis. This mixing of blocks of prose and poetry is a form he repeats in later volumes such as his "A Letter to God," but one which ultimately led to further experiments with prose poetry forms.

II *Simultaneity*

Both *The Journal of Albion Moonlight* and *Sleepers Awake* incorporate juxtaposed sections of prose and poetry in their multi-media (including drawing and concrete poetry) performance by the "total artist." The juxtaposition is carried a step further, however, through the formal innovation of simultaneity. Prose and poetry passages are printed in parallel juxtaposition on the page creating a simultaneous reading form. The goal is both audience engagement and psychological accuracy as these engaged texts force the audience to experience and find their own way through the mental chaos of multiple, often contradictory, messages. *Sleepers Awake* contains a twenty-five page section including simultaneous continuing messages of Irish lyric, large bold print prose, small bold print prose, and expressionistic line drawings, all running successively (pp. 236–260). The reader is literally forced to grapple alone with the poetry and prose messages creating his own experience and form.

Albion Moonlight contains more successful prose and poetry juxtapositions than *Sleepers Awake* as in the portion on the artist's duty. Here, Patchen proclaims: "It is the artist's duty to be alive."

To outflow the volcano in semen and phlegm		**GREEN GLINT**
To be treacherous when nothing is to be gained		**OF**
To enrich himself at the expense of everyone		**CHILDREN'S**
To reel in an exquisite sobriety	*I have no desire*	**VOICES AS**
To blush perpetually in gaping innocence	*to be intelligent*	**THEY PICK**
To drift happily through the ruined race-intelligence		**FLOWERS**
To burrow beneath the subconscious		
To defend the unreal at the cost of his reason	*I have*	
To obey each outrageous impulse	*no money*	
To commit his company to all enchantments	*whatever.*	
To rage against the sacrificing shepherds	*I can't*	
To return to a place remote from his native land	*make a*	
To pursue the languid executioner to his hall bedroom	*living*	
To torment the spirit-lice	*at all*	

(*Albion,* 255)

Even from this brief section, one can grasp the formal innovation, as Patchen captures a true stream of consciousness where multiple thoughts are entertained simultaneously. As one struggles to read and comprehend all three messages together, he experiences conflict, uneasiness, ambivalence, and yet some pervasive sense of continuity and freedom. To the confusion of personal metaphor contained in the statement of artistic duty is added the straightforward asides confessing simplicity and poverty, all compounded by the bold print message suggestive of a covert awareness of childlike wonder. Together they represent the true struggle of the artist, of Albion and Patchen in particular, who must perform a misunderstood duty, struggle with self (self-image and physical needs), and be constantly aware of the ready wonder ignored by the world. The juxtaposing is not random, but rather intuitive. The form gains its structure from the man himself, as the struggling consciousness of artist and audience strive to create an art "to happen" (*Albion,* 255).

III *Blending*

Patchen's next innovation with poetry and prose comes in his 1946 *Panels for the Walls of Heaven,* which he describes as "poems-in-prose."[1] The impulse is poetic and the form is prose. A mixture of media and not a true synthesis, the slim book is structurally and stylistically a composite — embracing paintings, crude picture-poems, concrete poetry, and the poems-in-prose. Using the panel motif (only one is actually titled "THE PANEL OF LONGING IN BEAUTY AND HORROR") Patchen creates an architectural structure containing various parts united in the book's whole — its common world view. Like a long panelled mural lining a corridor of heaven, Patchen's design provides a composite framework that adds resonance to each fragmented expression. It is an open structure which, like the book form for separate poems, is loose, fragmented, and groping. As in *Albion Moonlight* and *Sleepers Awake,* the form captures and evolves out of the artist's struggle to create in a dying world — the work's central theme. Lacking a core continuing narration, in its stead is the vague personal cohesiveness of the artist's creative act within a compelling world view. His later revision of these pieces into separate 'poems' for the *Collected Poems* with separate added titles and a new order further indicates such an awareness of composite form.

The poems-in-prose partake of this groping sense as they emerge as dark, almost black, visions of the world. It is as though the poetic impulse were unable to find a poetic form in such a spiritually dead world. Their lack of and struggle for form are reinforced by method and matter, as in this closing section:

> it is such a poor thing, this putting aimless marks on a paper when your soul is dead O what does it matter what bright juice oozes out of any head what does it matter how well the silken beautiful drums of art are thumped when all the long hideous whiteness of an everlasting void is stretched out here before us and if we cry God God ... and oh my pretty one my darling and all these sad majesties that live on the earth these lions and bears and doves these shores and thickets and the snow and the peaceful little wood ... there is such anguish in my heart there is black fear in me for all the world of God and man is dying and I have no place to take thee ...[2]

The language, the rhythms, the tone, the very impulse are all from poetry. The form is not so much prose as it is no form — no punctuation, no breaks, just one continual running together, as though the present world (the insane form) is sacrificing, even murdering, the art of today. Beside the lament for the "senseless marks" of art is the underlying awareness of spoiled wonder, of "all these sad majesties." This is Patchen's most anti-form experiment, but it is one he abandons after this work. It is used here because it dramatically symbolizes, in theme and feeling, the artist's struggle against the crisis of the world's spiritual death.

IV   *Synthesis*

The two works that suggest Patchen's arrival at a successful poetry prose synthesis are *The Famous Boating Party* (1954) and *Poemscapes* (1958) — his prose poems. Both works come when Patchen is increasingly turning to wonder for theme and form, when imaginative and unrational celebrations are his chief thematic content; yet each is a unique work in itself. Though varied in tones, both books demonstrate Patchen's uniquely American innovation of humor to the prose poem form.

The Famous Boating Party is filled with the speech cadences, the imagery, and the figurative language of poetry. The motivational key to this prose poem development seems to lie in Patchen's desire to create a viable form where a variety of personae could speak their own poems. There are the young, the old, brawlers and boasters, lovers and lawyers, story tellers and Patchen's special wonder people who speak the crazy language of riddles and fun. To capture the oral feel of the form Patchen uses the titles as the speaker's initial address which runs on through the remainder of the poem: "NOW IF YOU / Do it just right, anything will grow" (*C.P.* 444). Or in this little prose poem of hope:

SOON IT WILL

Be showtime again. Somebody will paint beautiful faces all over the sky. Somebody will start bombarding us with really wonderful letters ... letters full of truth, and gentleness, and humility

... Soon (it says here) ... (*C.P.* 437)

The reader is immediately launched into the flow of speech, here in a statement which we belatedly learn is being read aloud to us "(it says here)."

Many of these poems from colorful and talkative personae were later recorded by Patchen to jazz or solo.[3] As John Peale Bishop early recognized, Patchen's "poetic speech is contemporary and close to the streets."[4] Patchen's vernacular ear for American street language prompts him to create the prose poem form to capture such life reflected in speech. The effects range from absurdly humorous to touchingly serious, but it is always Patchen's world of madness, love, and wonder that is reflected in these plebian mirrors. In "The Great-Sledmakers," Patchen creates his own imaginative myth through the slightly crazed persona who informs us:

They get drunk, these Great-Sledmakers. Their copper mugs, around which their fingers easily circle once, and once again, hold what's called a "quart handsome" (about five and 3/8ths gallon mirke-measure). The Great-Sledmakers get drunk like other people do hopeless. An hour or two old they demand whisky, and poor slaphoppy brute the mother who'd not lay them lovely on ... all pink-fuzzy, ah happy little belchers, rest ye well in between worlds, as you might say. (*C.P.* 442)

The persona reveals himself as he becomes more verbally loose, sliding in and out of asides, using contractions, and devising his own words. The total effect is one of happy release as Patchen allows the jovial narrator to make his own wonder myth, ending with a call for more "Whh-isky, bo-oy!" (*C.P.* 443).

In "Court of First Appeal," the language of legal jargon is infused with the life breath of poetic wonder talk as Patchen's persona declares his belief,

> In the splendorment and holification of every thing individuated,
> and of every thing togetherized; from causes known to me, from
> causes forever (unassailably) unknown to me: I believe! (*C.P.* 459)

Here the speech cadences combine with the poetic reinforcement of word creation to make a sworn statement of life's unified serenity. Legal logic is ironically placed in the context of Patchen's own unreasoning logic of wonder.

Perhaps the most effective poem of this volume is "That Night The," which uses the persona of remembered youth passing through adolescent awareness. Imagery and speech rhythms are fully poetic and yet quietly authentic. The prose poem seems to be spoken from the young boy's heart as he tells of the night the "Moon came out full, you could see the white breathing of the / fields down by the swimming hole" (*C.P.* 446) where the night's cool air "was like having cool, moist hands touch your face, you could smell the sweat rising up off the fields" (*C.P.* 446). To this archetypal and impressionistic rendering of time and place is added the boyish humor of youth:

> The boy who worked the next field said to my brother, "Them's my
> goddam feet you're a-splashin' 'baccy juice on."
>
> I knew that my champion water-drinker of a brother had run out of cut-
> plug long before supper, but I didn't say anything." (*C.P.* 446)

To this self-portrait of youthful sensitivity and good camaraderie, the persona adds in profound and simplistic sincerity the final awareness:

> After while there come the town girls out of the pool to get dressed ... All
> shiny wet — like little soft pink and white fish ... Oh jesus they was all
> sorta crazy pretty ... And we ground our broken nails into our fists,
> hating them. (*C.P.* 446)

The moving expression of the boy's struggle to give words and form to that lost time, when awaiting sex stirred through his young body with ambivalent love and hate, allow the poetry inherent in the boy and the moment to surface in an apt synthesis of poetry and prose. Like other American adolescent heroes, this youth seeks to express what we have all forgotten or denied in adulthood. Like Huck Finn, George Willard, Gene Gant, Nick Adams, and Holden Caulfield, he speaks in prose the poetry of emotion lying below the muted surface of life. Patchen has created a form to present common expression of the daily poetry of our lives. It is a form he continues to use in later volumes including the love lyrics of *When We Were Here Together.*

In *Poemscapes,* however, Patchen gives the prose poem a new function and a unique form. Taking the book's title on its simplest level, it would seem to indicate poem views of life, and the poems are indeed that. The book is one of Patchen's most philosophical, and he seeks in each short verse to paint in more of the world he viewed. If, however, Patchen's title bears any relationship to Gerard Manley Hopkins' term "inscapes," then the poemscapes would also embrace the definition of momentary illuminations of the inner workings of the essence of things. Both definitions fit quite well together, as Patchen seeks to expose and explain his world in this unique form. The book's cover notes, apparently written by publisher Jonathan Williams, declare, "*Poemscapes* is a door flung open on the innermost world of the poet."[5] Frederick Eckman adds an explanatory description of the book as "made up, rather like a book of hours or a breviary, into fifty-two 'poemscapes' — each consisting of four short prose poems."[6] Williams' insight to the book's interrelationship with the poet's world and Eckman's analogy to the prayer books both seem consistent and appropriate. Indeed, one of the demands of this work is for an immersion in the Patchen world; it cannot be read with understanding any other way.

Patchen's world view is the familiar one, however. There is the warning declamation on societal madness, as in "THE MODERN SICKNESS": "On every hand there is a nasty slyness, a petty viciousness; not to serve any purpose really, ... A nothing-for-nothing affair; petty, nasty, vicious — a sort of vegetarian cannibalism."[7] There is the open statement on love:

1) FASHIONED IN LOVE

Let it be fashioned in love! Boundless and imperturbable. Let it be! O tiger sleeping in the rose heart. Let it be! Masterless, remote solitary. A country where men and birds may come to take breath. (*Poemscapes, #*I)

Mixed with the declaration of love are suggested wonder images of "tiger sleeping in the rose heart." To which Patchen openly declares in his prayerful "LIFE IS PRAISE": "O unto me be given praising's gift! Wonder and love! O wonder and love!" (*Poemscapes, #*I). In this book of Patchen cosmology are his basic beliefs in a unity of life, a world brotherhood, in the sentience of all things, and in the flowing essence of existence: "Because all appearances have a common origin in the unseeable fluidity *which issues forth from the action of its own flowing*" (*Poemscapes, #*XXX). The further Patchen goes into his world of wonder, the more he requires a new kind of thinking. In its form and content *Poemscapes* is designed to *teach* this new approach to life.

Though Patchen is rarely recognized for his formal abilities, many of his poemscapes appeared originally in the conservative and formally excellent *Poetry* magazine. Eckman compares them with the experimental work of William Carlos Williams in *Kora in Hell: Improvisations* and finds "their imagery is more exotic and their pattern somewhat more formal."[8] The comparison is revealing, for both works share a conscious design to express new bits of wisdom in a newer, freer, and more viable form. Patchen holds a keen interest in form, particularly when it can be used to reinforce his reforms. Jonathan Williams identifies one of the formal principles of this work as Patchen's concern for "controlled freedom."[9] This "controlled freedom" is expressed by Patchen as a kind of gentle guidance that allows the form to find itself. To explain this view of organic form he makes an analogy with the creative act: "Those who work with their hands know that the proper method for moving a heavy stone is to get a good firm hold, brace your feet, kick it into motion with the nubs of your fists, and ride it to where you want it to go. Make the stone work. . . . This is another way of saying that my interest in structure is great."[10]

When the poemscape gets in touch with the flowing existence, the poet responds by creatively helping it to flow:

33) YOUNG GIRLS SWIMMING

Bodies like wavering, half-dissolving flowers, young girls swimming in the river. There! the pink, silken petal of a thigh! the clustering loveliness of a tiny breast! How very blue and pure the sky above them. (*Poemscapes,* #IX)

The act of perception, the scape, prompts the gentle flow of image relationships. Very much like the Imagist school of poetry, the goal is to capture in concise accuracy the reality of the thing itself. It is that momentary illumination captured by all the poet's tools, from his sensitivity to his ability with prose cadences and poetic images to get it down. This explains the individual style and tone of the varied poemscapes which differ so radically from each other; each partakes of the essence of the thing itself. Later, for example, we have one of Patchen's angered ejaculations:

167) YOU'RE ALL NUTS

Boobs, scamps, frauds, and all you assorted blaugh-swilling drearies — oh, COME OFF IT! (*Poemscapes,* #XLII)

Namecalling, appropriate to his violent perception of the fraudulent activity of life, guides the form. Prose and poetry rhythms are used together in the staccato conciseness that accentuates the awareness. Patchen believed: "There is such a thing as weight to words. A rhythm felt is a rhythm that has its own laws."[11] Like the prose poem form of *The Famous Boating Party* where the form fits the persona, the form found in *Poemscapes* accurately captures the inner reality of the perceptive act.

A second motivation behind the prose poem form is that of mutual reinforcement. Jonathan Williams finds this functional design in agreement with the book's overall purpose of instructing and of explaining reality. Prose resonance is added to poetic impulse: "Something of the native textures, the dynamic and unselfconscious flow of its prose rhythms, has been brought over to enrich and deepen the necessarily more confined expression of verbal means, without sacrifice of either the music or the emotional coloring."[12] Like Eastern wisdom statements, or the prayers of any religion, poetic conciseness and emotional responsiveness combine with prose flow to give the views a moving sense of significance and permanence. They are the holy words of Patchen's beliefs. Combining most of these characteristics is the example of:

GOLDEN PLUM BUDS (50

Since it is as beautiful as it is, there will be nothing done in vain in this world. When it lay across my hand, the ardent glow of noon upon it, reverently, barely touching it, as a golden mouth lightly touches a forehead fashioned of cobwebs, I seemed to have entered an unsuspected portal. (*Poemscapes,* #XIII)

To the flowing prose are added the quiet, responsive music and imagery of poetry. The phrasing of the second line in particular partakes of the short, simple, yet emotional expression of verse. Like Japanese poetry, the act of perception and the act of expression are fused in sincere and simple impulse. In images of a "golden mouth" touching "a forehead fashioned of cobwebs" the reader too is imperceptibly swept into the "unsuspected portal" of quiet and profound awareness. Like the best of William Carlos Williams or Wallace Stevens' poetry, the poem rings with the very "rightness" of the expression.

Poemscapes, a book of stunning formal achievements as well as troubled failures, contains Patchen's fullest synthesis of poetry and prose. Startling in its diversity of style, tone, and theme, the work's unity rests in Patchen's design to capture his world vision and to instruct others in the *way.*

CHAPTER 8

Concrete Poetry

KENNETH Patchen's poetry is so diverse — ranging from tough street protest to tender love lyric, from comic creature fables to mystical meditation, from sonnets to jazz poetry — so that its visionary and experimental nature emerges as the only general characteristics. Four unique areas of formal experimentation stand out: early developments with concrete poetry, a progressive synthesis of poetry and jazz, irrational tales and verse, and the culminating formal fusion of poetry and painting. All his poetry is predicated on his theory of a functional, engaged, and intuitive art. Most also reflects his continued pursuit of the joint ideals of the "total artist" and the "total book." Each experimental area further reveals the man and his art.

As a part of the Dadaist Movement of the early twentieth century, Concrete Art turned to physical reality and concrete forms of expression in hopes of saving man from his dangerous reliance on reason and abstractions. The Concrete Poetry Movement, which emerged in the early 1950's as the belated and developed child of the Concrete Art Movement, bears striking resemblances in theory and practice to its predecessor. Patchen as an early original experimenter in concrete poetry assumes a position of intermediary, developing original concrete poetic forms to fulfill the functional demands of concrete art. Hans Arp's manifesto on "Concrete Art" applies to and reveals the goals of all three movements: "concrete art aims to transform the world. it aims to make existence more bearable. it aims to save man from the most dangerous folly: vanity. it aims to simplify man's life. it aims to identify him with nature. reason uproots man and causes him to lead a tragic existence. concrete art is elemental, natural, healthy art, which causes the stars of peace, love and poetry to grow in the head and heart."[1] Patchen's own goals of a world-transforming art are expressed

113

accurately and concisely here, as he too sought to cure mankind of its displaced existence from man's vain faith in reason. Concrete art, concrete poetry, and Kenneth Patchen's works each seek in parallel ways to restore humanity to peace and love by reestablishing man to nature through an art of concrete forms.

Mary Ellen Solt's *Concrete Poetry: A World View* contains the essence of this international movement's theory and art, from which we can gain a general understanding of the movement for a basic understanding of Patchen's concrete verse. Concrete poetry itself embraces a wide diversity of forms within a common basis of theory. The reduced elements of language are the concrete poet's tools for capturing concrete forms of experience: "Generally speaking the material of the concrete poem is language: words reduced to their elements of letters (to see) syllables (to hear). Some concrete poets stay with whole words. Others find fragments of letters or individual speech sounds more suited to their needs. The essential is *reduced language*."[2] Solt continues this definition and description by recognizing the two basic approaches of sight poetry and sound poetry. She further reveals their analogies to the sister arts of painting and music: "The concrete poet is concerned with establishing his linguistic materials in a new relationship to space (the page or its equivalent) and/or to time (abandoning the old linear measure). Put another way this means the concrete poet is concerned with making an object to be perceived rather than read. The visual poem is intended to be seen like a painting; the sound poem is composed to be listened to like music."[3] Such a theory is clearly consistent with Patchen's own view that art should "happen" for an audience. It is therefore understandable to find him experimenting whith both visual and sound poetry and to see him creating true concrete poetry some ten years before the Concrete Poetry Movement took form.

Patchen's relationship to the Movement of Concrete Poetry has never been clearly defined for various reasons. Though he proclaims in his 1969 pamphlet *Kenneth Patchen: Painter of Poems,* "Kenneth Patchen is the originator of the form of poetry which uses the modern printing press as the instrument of creation. . . . His efforts have resulted in a number of spinoff activities variously called concrete poetry, visual poetry, or poetry of the printed press,"[4] generally his concrete contributions go unrecognized by the movement. One reason for this lack of acknowledgment is that

Patchen's experiments in concrete poetry were completed before the movement formally began. Solt charts the history of the movement as a post World War II phenomenon that received its initial thrust from Eugen Gomringer's *Constellations* in 1953, from the joint efforts of the Brazilian Noigandres group, and from Oyvind Fahlstrom's "Manifesto for konkret poesie," also published in 1953.[5] By the mid-1950's various international artists began to recognize shared goals and practices associated with concrete poetry. Patchen's concrete poetry, however, first appeared in *Cloth of the Tempest* (1943), followed by the bulk of his concrete work in *Sleepers Awake* and *Panels for the Walls of Heaven,* both published in 1946. Though his poetry-painting experiments embrace many of the principles of concrete poetry, Patchen did not continue to produce concrete verse after 1946.

Other reasons why the Movement may have chosen to ignore Patchen's work are readily at hand. They may have been embarrassed by his early mature experiments; it may also be true that his experiments — published obscurely in equally obscure books — simply were not read. The Concrete Poetry Movement does recognize early predecessors in the art "from Mallarmé through Joyce-Pound-Cummings,"[6] and Solt claims such other American pre cursors as Gertrude Stein, William Carlos Williams, Charles Olson, Louis Zukofsky, and even Whitman for his long cataloguing technique. Recognized contemporaries of Solt's are Robert Creeley, Jonathan Williams, Emmett Williams, and Ronald Johnson.[7] Only Jonathan Williams, Patchen's friend and publisher, acknowledges the influence of Patchen's work on the Movement.[8] It thus appears that Patchen's concrete poetry preceded and paralleled the Movement, though it remained a separate and as yet unappreciated development of the art.

In theory the Movement defines itself as a functionally designed art. Max Bense, the German concrete poet, affirms simply that "All art is concrete which uses its material functionally and not symbolically."[9] The Brazilian Noigandres group defines art as "total responsibility before language.... A general art of the word. The poem-product: useful object."[10] Although it is a "useful object," it is never merely a tool for propaganda, but rather an art form integral with the needs of modern life. Solt clarifies this functional aesthetics so comparable with Patchen's: "The concrete poem finds itself isolated in space to make a significance of its given materials as contemporary man finds himself isolated in space to make a significance of his life."[11] Letters and sounds, as models, appear on the page in functional and meaningful relationships with each other and space. It is a form which shares man's pattern of existence as well as relevant insights into that pattern. As Emmett Williams explains: "It was born of the times, as a way of knowing and saying something about the world of *now,* with the techniques and insights of *now.*"[12]

Among those modern techniques is the technology of printing devices employed in concrete verse to reveal and humanize themselves. When a machine like the computer or the printing press is used to make something beautiful, that machine also becomes beautiful. Though the instruments and the elements of concrete poetry may be radically new, the aesthetics are basic: "All definitions of concrete poetry can be reduced to the same formula: form = content/content = form."[13] Like Patchen's view of art, function and form unite as all art is working, and all that is working is art. In this theory from a movement which followed him, Patchen's own view of art is accurately expressed. Eugen Gomringer's words declare Patchen's own goals as poet-prophet: "The aim of the new poetry is to give poetry an organic function in society again, and in doing so to restate the position of the poet in society."[14] And the theory leads to a consideration of the practice.

Lacking a formal tradition of concrete poetics and models, Patchen's own experiments embrace a wide variety of forms and functions shared by later concrete poets. In his effort to create a "total book," conceived, created, and controlled by one man, he took on the skills of typography to paint with print. The visual poems that result are both the emotive experiments of expressionism and the functional concrete designs of poetry. In *Sleepers Awake* for example, he creates a series of five expressionist poems using marble shaped dots and various sizes of type. In the portion reproduced below the treatment and effect are those of his later picture-poems. It is an emotive poster poem:

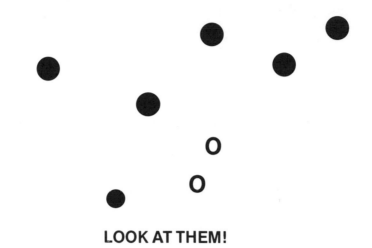

LOOK AT THEM!

See how they go up!

What do they care about darkness!

(*Sleepers,* 225)

These expressionist print experiments which include typographical symbols, various sizes of type, and juxtaposed printing of prose and poetry represent one avenue of his development. Many are print paintings but not actual concrete poems. However, the distinction is a vague one, as is demonstrated in a later poem, "SEVEN BEAUTIFUL THINGS / MADE MORE BEAUTIFUL BY APPEARING / IN THIS WAY" from *Sleepers Awake.* Title alone indicates Patchen's awareness of concrete functional aesthetics, and the poem demonstrates this principle by including expressionist phrases in assorted type faces and varying positions on the page, and with a random numbering. For example:

3. Colt and huge red stones.

7. A gean floating on bark.

5. Cloud-mold lying on wet grass.

2. The sound of mountains.

6. You put one here.

(*Sleepers,* 231)

The reduced language of phrases combined with sight and sound forms make the poem in part an act of perception. Typographically, he is painting concretely and expressionistically. Following the dictates of concrete poetry, as Claus Bremer describes the genre: "It yields a process of discovery. It is motion. Its motion ends in different readers in different ways."[15] By inviting the reader to "put one here," to add his own image phrase, Patchen acknowledges the need for reader participation on an individual level, an approach he will expand on.

In his "Manifesto for a New Poetry — Visual and Phonic," Pierre Garnier asserts the concrete artist's demand for creative perception: "A word which is read only grazes, the reader's mind: but a word that is perceived, or accepted, starts off a chain of reactions there."[16] This formulation has led concrete poets to a theory of "engaged texts," those formal techniques which force the reader to visually and sometimes physically — through mechanical manipulation of the page — participate in the creative act of perception.

Claus Bremer writes of his concrete poems: "These are not engaging texts. They are engaged texts.... This text, as do all my engaged texts, sets the reader free in the realm of his own possibilities, the realm in which we are brothers."[17] Patchen's art, as already demonstrated, is passionately dedicated to this ideal of audience engagement. His formal experiments with engaged texts are extensive, and his goal is as spiritually motivated as Bremer's or Garnier's: "I shock the French reader, I take him out of his element, I force him to re-examine the language and, in this way, the world."[18]

Patchen's untitled poem on page fifty-three of *Panels*[19] illustrates one of his characteristic engaged forms. Including typographical variety and a functional sense of linguistic elements, the work is interspliced horizontally and vertically. Words are not spaced as expected, and they break unnaturally by line. This puzzling maze of letters requires a concentrated effort at comprehension. To the deliberate act of perception is added the gradual organic unfolding of meaning. Thus perception of form and awareness of meaning are welded in the simultaneous act of reading — an engaged act of author, art, and audience. A few pages later, Patchen provides the concrete poem "THE NATURE OF REALITY / THE REALITY OF NATURE" which looks like American Indian iconography, where single words and images are allowed to establish relationships in meaning and form by their positioning. Similarly, objects and concepts are linked in a spiritual message of significance.

(SEE NEXT PAGE FOR CONCRETE POEM)

Analysis and synthesis as well as aesthetic perception are tools required of the engaged reader involved in this concrete poem.

In other forms demanding engaged reading Patchen more closely identifies perception of form and meaning. *Sleepers Awake* contains many pages of concrete poetry such as:

(SEE NEXT PAGE FOR CONCRETE POEM)

THE NATURE OF REALITY

Bed.   Apple.

    Sly bird.   Policeman.

       Famine.   Rod of milk.

        Dice.   Groan.

         Stone.   Towel.

         Divot.

"Put some on mine."   Six or Tad Prichard.

THE REALITY OF NATURE

       Seeking

     death   life

    growth   decay

   peace   madness

  conflict   silence

birth   dissolution

"Put some in me."   Tad Prichard or none.

(*Panels* in *Quest*, 58)

DEA^TH

LO^OK'N^G

^DOO^N

(*Sleepers,* 148)

Here each letter and word — in size and position — suggest the impression as well as the perception of the word concept. The diminutive "TH" of death suggests distance, either rationalized or remotely conceived; the searching that the eyes make as they go "looking" and find themselves in the visual eyeballs of 'down' and the resonant sinking sound of "OO" are all functionally concrete. On the following page Patchen presents the reader with a typographical explosion entitled "BooM" which contains a scattering of letters arranged in loose vertical reading order and followed by a cry of "help" which goes screaming down the left margin in a succession of twenty-five exclamations. This sight and sound pattern is later repeated in the equally spaced cry of sixteen vertical printings of "DOWN WITH ALL GOVERNMENTS," which is only interrupted by the darkly printed explanatory message of "one little man running about shouting" (*Sleepers*, 215).

The methods of concrete poetry seem to adapt equally well to Patchen's acid attacks on social madness. The feel of such a poem is that of an initial visual perception of the page — as if it were a painting — followed by a gradual awareness of meaning and form reinforced by an audial reading. All aspects are realized through the engaged reading which the form demands. Patchen adds to this the sense of a continued flow onto the next page, as each concrete poem is incorporated into the total framework of the book. Instead of neat one page poems, there is a larger form within a kinetic book. Perhaps this is the most appropriate way of treating Patchen's *Sleepers Awake* and *Panels for the Walls of Heaven,* as sequential material that emerges organically as a flow of energy derived from the material itself and from the creative act of perception.

One of Patchen's earliest and most clearly concrete poems is "The Murder of Two Men by a Young Kid / Wearing Lemon-colored Gloves." Printed in the 1943 *Cloth of the Tempest,* the text is a series of the word "Wait" appearing in an intuitive and expressionistic pattern down the page. It cannot be read without the requisite dramatic and oral feel as the brief and fearful cries form a visual scuffle upon the page, climaxing in the terrible finality of:

(SEE NEXT PAGE FOR CONCRETE POEM)

Wait.

                                  Wait.

                                      Wait.

                Wait.

                                    Wait.

Wait.

        NOW.

                                      (C.P. 293)

The whole experience is communicated and recreated by the reader in this classic piece of audial concrete. At the time it must have been regarded as play, but it is the kind of useful play that Eugen Gomringer claims for concrete poetry: "So the new poem is simple and can be perceived visually as a whole as well as parts. It becomes an object to be both seen and used: an object containing thought but made concrete through play-activity.... Its objective element of play is useful to modern man."[21]

Patchen realized this play could also be used to help man better perceive his world, as a means of indicating earthly beauty and the world's potential to inspire wonder. This aim is demonstrated in another of his classic concrete poems:

                (SEE NEXT PAGE FOR CONCRETE POEM)

Incorporated in the kinetic flow of *Sleepers Awake,* this poem epitomizes the concrete use of reduced language, single letters and phonemes ("ngngngngngng"), to both paint and play on verbal connotations. As the word "shining" is realized by the reader, the visual letter pattern and corresponding sound play reinforce each other. The "s" hushes down the "h" and rises in delight with the "i" then winds around "n" and "i" ending in a happy awareness. The word "sing" is also suggested in content and form, and the diagonal pattern of a large "N" reinforces the appropriateness of

```
s                        the sun was              i
h  s                     n   n   n   n   n        i
h    s                     n   n   n   n          i
h      s                 n   n   n   n   n         i
h        s                 n   n   n   n           i
h  i  i     s            n   n   n   n   n         i
h  i  i       s            n   n   n   n           i
h          i  i   s                               i
h          i  i     s                             i
h                     s                           i
h     ngngngngngng        s                       i
h     ngngngngngng          s                     i
h     ngngngngngng            s                   i
h     ngngngngngng              s                 i
h     ngngngngngng                s               i
h     ngngngngngng                  s             i
h                                     s   i
h                                         i
```

(*Sleepers,* 213)

form as perception and emotion combine in the awareness of joy.

A technique of "fascination" integral with Patchen's view of life and art is extolled by poet Max Bense: "Concrete poetry does not entertain. It holds the possibility of fascination, and fascination is a form of concentration, that is of concentration which includes

perception of the material as well as apperception of its meaning."[22] The design and effect of this "shining" poem is that of true
concrete poetry — a calculated sight-sound-mind perception. It
serves as a useful instrument in leading man to recognize the wonder of his own senses and mind as well as that of the world. As a
poet practicing outside the organized movement, Patchen's output
of concrete poetry is prodigious and unprecedented.[23] The art of
Kenneth Patchen and the art of Concrete Poetry are thus mutually
revealing.

CHAPTER 9

Poetry-and-Jazz

D URING the late 1950's the Poetry-and-Jazz Movement
evolved on the West Coast. Having a precedent of five centuries in the Renaissance practice of reading poetry to music in cel-
lars, this modern movement represented the contemporary synthesis of brother art forms — jazz music and free verse. It was a
"natural" in that artists outside the mainstream of society, especially jazzmen and experimental poets, have long studied and influenced each other. Both jazz music and contemporary poetry
have evolved forms based on intuitive improvisation and emotional
flow (whether "hot" or "cool"), and both create an art that fosters
free expression of angry social protest as well as tender love. Based
on the artist's personal expression of contemporary life, these
brother arts seek to offer the world a reflection of itself. As a pioneer and main force in this movement, Kenneth Patchen achieves
within his concept of the "total artist" a synthesis of poetry and
jazz, an engaging art form that is actively performed upon its
audience. An understanding of Patchen's place in this varied and
poorly chronicled period of American literature can illuminate
both his art and the Poetry-and-Jazz Movement itself.

The history of the movement is surrounded by misconceptions,
the chief one being the popular but limited association with Beat
poetry. In reality, it is a varied movement grounded on a deep
appreciation of jazz rather than the disillusion and nihilism of the
Beats. Its main figures are three of the main forces of the whole San
Francisco Renaissance in poetry — Kenneth Rexroth, Kenneth
Patchen, and Lawrence Ferlinghetti. Though Patchen denied
membership in the San Francisco or any other regional movement,
he was a force in the very atmosphere of San Francisco, as the poets
themselves testify.

All three of these dominant figures in poetry-and-jazz had a long association with jazz itself. Long before poetry-and-jazz appeared in 1956, both Rexroth and Patchen had studied and written on jazz. In his journalistic writings of explanation and suggested listening, Rexroth had attempted to bring that kind of music to a wider audience.[1] Patchen's references are more obscurely printed than the critical essays of Rexroth, but both are impressively full. In "AND IN ANOTHER PLACE USES THE SAME PHRASES" from the 1939 *First Will and Testament* Patchen includes as part of the surreal cast of characters in this poem-play a list of jazz musicians from the early 1920's and 1930's. Mentioned are Bix Biederbeck, Mike Gibbons, Bat Nelson, Pretty Amberg, and Bob Fitzsimmons (*C.P.* 120–21). Suggested titles include: "Wabash Blues," "Tin Roof," and "Basin Street," followed by a list of prominent jazz-men of the 1930's: Red Allen, Cozy Cole, Ziggy Elman, and a salutory reference to Louis Armstrong as "Louis The One and Only put that big train on through the night" (*C.P.* 122). By 1942 the jazz influence is more direct on Patchen's poetry as he works lyrics from "Midnight Special" into his poems (*C.P.* 177). *Sleepers Awake* sings of "see see rider, see what you have done" and of "O careless love . . ." (*Sleepers,* 216). The most complete reference to jazz background, however, appears in the 1945 *Memoirs of a Shy Pornographer,* where Patchen promotes jazz with a two page listing of "the disks you'll have to get if you want a basic jazz library" (*Memoirs,* 56). Complete song and band titles are listed, indicating a thorough familiarity with early jazz:

> *Snake Rag,* by King Oliver and his Creole Band.
> *Dixie Jass Band One-Step,* by the Original Dixieland Jazz Band.
> *Maple Leaf Rag,* by the New Orleans Rhythm Kings. . . .
> *Mahogany Hall Stomp,* by Louis Armstrong and his Orchestra.
> *The Chant,* by Jelly-Roll Morton and his Red Hot Peppers.
> *See-See Rider,* by Ma Rainey. . . .
> *Lazy Daddy, Dat Street Car's Comin' Long,* by Big Rabbit Gary's Plantation Boys. (*Memoirs,* 57–8).

Such a list reflects an acute awareness of jazz discography and expresses Patchen's ear for the poetry of popular culture. Like Whitman's use of place names in America, Patchen's titles sing of the cultural reality and common poetry of early jazz. From such an interest and awareness of early jazz roots grew the poetry-and-jazz movement.

I *Poetry-and-Jazz Chronicle*

Historically Rexroth, Patchen, and Ferlinghetti all claim and deserve recognition for the pioneer role each played in the movement's development. Rexroth indicates his early experimentation with poetry-and-jazz recitals done with Langston Hughes in a small Chicago club during the 1930's.[2] Ferlinghetti made early experimental tapes of his poetry to jazz readings.[3] Patchen's own innovative work began with the 1951 tapes of his reading his fables with a jazz recording background. Carolyn See credits Patchen with this early experiment in her revealing study of "The Jazz Musician as Patchen's Hero,"[4] and Jonathan Williams verifies it in his account of the tapes made by two of Patchen's young Harvard admirers. The fables were taped to "the Bunk Johnson and George Lewis records that Bill Russell was sending from Chicago. (A little later, it was these LPs that Patchen used in making private tapes of the fables. All kinds of home-made noises and jazz were interpolated back of the voice.... They were, to my knowledge, the first instances of the later poetry/jazz experiment.)"[5]

The movement did not begin publicly, however, until the autumn of 1956 when "tapes of Patchen reading to jazz records" were broadcast on the C.B.C. radio network.[6] The movement's blossoming year was 1957 when Ferlinghetti and Rexroth first performed their poetry-and-jazz readings that spring in The Cellar, a small San Francisco club. Their historic performances were recorded live that year by Fantasy Records as *Poetry Readings in "The Cellar."* *Time* magazine caught wind of the movement and printed an article "The Cool, Cool Bards" (Dec. 2, 1957) which listed besides Rexroth, Ferlinghetti, and Patchen, the poet Kenneth Ford and saxaphonist-poet Bruce Lippincott as early West Coast innovators. The clubs promoting poetry-and-jazz were centered in San Francisco and included the Sail'n, the Blackhawk (where Patchen first appeared), and The Cellar.

Jazz musicians were, on the whole, wary about this new movement which they had not initiated. Those offering sympathy and support, however, included Dave Brubeck, Judy and Lennie Tristano, Sonny Wayne and Bill Weisjahns (owners of The Cellar), trumpeter Dickie Mills and Bruce Moore (who played with Rexroth), The Cellar Jazz Quintet (who played with Rexroth and Ferlinghetti), Charlie Mingus (who played with Rexroth, Langston

Hughes, and later with Patchen), and Allyn Ferguson's Chamber
Jazz Sextet (which later played and recorded with Patchen).[7] As
Carolyn See suggests, the jazz musical environment of the late
1950's evolved "from the 'bebop' school of Dizzy Gillespie to the
'cool' sound of Miles Davis and Lennie Tristano, Lee Konitz, and
the whole legend of Charlie Parker."[8] Jazz of that time thus included a diversity of "hot" and "cool," East and West, white and
black sounds. Poetry-and-Jazz was responsive to this diversity of
emotional and cerebral expression by providing an equal diversity
of forms and approaches.

By 1958 other poets and musicians had joined the movement. In
May Patchen released his first recording, *Kenneth Patchen Reads
with the Chamber Jazz Sextet* (Cadence, 3004). World Pacific
released *Jazz Canto, Vol. I: An Anthology of Jazz & Poetry*
(WP-1244), which included Philip Whalen and Ferlinghetti. These
recordings along with performing tours gave the movement a wider
audience. Patchen toured the United States and Canada performing at clubs, concerts, and campuses, as did Rexroth. John Ciardi
records a successful engagement of Patchen's at New York's classic
Five Spot cafe, thus indicating that poetry-and-jazz had been carried to the East Coast.

By 1959 Patchen had spread the movement through a two month
engagement at Los Angeles Jazz Concert Hall, an appearance on
Hollywood television's "Stars of Jazz," a Seattle concert, and
tours of college campuses. Besides his appearance at the Five Spot,
Patchen read at New York's Living Theater with Charlie Mingus,
where his jazz-play *Don't Look Now* was scheduled to begin.[9]
Of equal significance was an engagement in February 1959 at Vancouver's Cellar club. At that time, Patchen and Alan Neil's Quartet
recorded *Kenneth Patchen Reads with Jazz in Canada* (Folkways,
FL9718). This recording, which was broadcast on the Montreal
radio in October, represents the highest and truest achievement of
the poetry-and-jazz synthesis. Other writers who became involved
in the movement were Jack Kerouac, who released an album with
Al Cohn and Zoot Sims: *Jack Kerouac: Blues and Haikus*
(Hanover, HM 5906) in 1959 and Kenneth Koch who with artist
Larry Rivers set out to parody the movement at the Five Spot, but
turned their performance into a successful living experience.[10]

For Patchen, 1959 held public acclaim as well as personal
tragedy. After years of suffering, Patchen received another spinal

fusion. In preparation for additional exploratory surgery he accidentally slipped from the table, severely damaging his spine. This "surgical mishap" resulted in continued physical pain and confinement at his Palo Alto, California home for the remainder of his life. He had to cease performing, except on record, and the whole Poetry-and-Jazz Movement seemed to settle. A barrage of poor imitations followed, trying to capitalize on the art form in small clubs and coffee houses, while the active sincere adherents led their new audiences into further experiments with poetry. The Movement did not die, however; gradually it became less of a novelty and more of an accepted permanent contribution to literature and music. Besides creating an original art form, it had won a new and larger audience for both poetry and jazz music. *New Jazz Poets* (BR461), edited by Walter Lowenfels and released by Folkways in 1967, testifies to continued experimentation with the synthesis of poetry and jazz; poets such as Ishmael Reed, Paul Blackburn, John Morgan, Peter LaFarge, and Joel Oppenheimer record their modern art form of jazz poetry.

II *A Diversity of Approaches*

To grasp both the scope of the movement and Patchen's particular place within the collaborative genre, it is necessary to compare briefly the varied treatments of the poetry-and-jazz experiment by its leading figures. Three friends whose poetry shares a common view of the world but whose forms are strongly individualized — Rexroth, Ferlinghetti, and Patchen — thus represent three different yet related approaches to the art of poetry-and-jazz.

The chief motivation for the movement as expressed by Ferlinghetti and Rexroth was to give poetry a wider audience. Rexroth exclaims, "Poetry is a dying art in modern civilization. Poetry and jazz together return the poet to his audience."[11] Ferlinghetti explains, "The poets today are talking to themselves, they have no other audience. The competition with the mass media is too much.... We're trying to capture an audience.... The jazz comes in as part of an attempt to get the audience back."[12] Patchen varies here in the degree of his motivational direction. Although all three sought a larger audience for poetry, Patchen's primary motivation was with the creation of the new art form. Though he worked harder than any of the others to propagate the form, he also was more successful than they in synthesizing poetry and jazz. Whereas Rexroth and Ferlinghetti achieve "poetry-and-jazz," Patchen achieves the ideal of "poetry-jazz."

Rexroth's early experiments with the mixed media constitute a series of comparisons and analogies between his early poems and corresponding jazz pieces. Carolyn See explains how Rexroth "draws the parallel between a poem he reads about an Oriental courtesan waiting for the man she loves, and who never comes, and the old blues chants of Ma Rainey and other Negro singers — but usually the comparison is specious."[13] Rexroth simply adds a jazz context to an earlier poem written without music in mind. However, in his most effective piece, "Thou Shalt Not Kill — (In memory of Dylan Thomas)," Rexroth has created a form designed for jazz. This angry poem, written in contemporary street speech, better serves the poetry-and-jazz form and function, though it still achieves only a paralleling effect. Bruce Lippincott, musician for both Rexroth and Ferlinghetti, explains the "free-form jazz" approach they used: "We set up the first rule — listen to each other. And second — respond with our instruments as emotionally as possible to the *words* of the poem and also the pre-arranged form.... If we listen to each other we can get a kind of question and answer thing going on underneath, all without any key. It comes down to a different approach to jazz, in a way."[14] This tack certainly allows for some creativity; the only thing prearranged was when the instruments would come in. Its weakness is that the word dominates — it becomes a jazz accompaniment to a poetry reading. Juxtaposition is not synthesis.

Lawrence Ferlinghetti offers another approach. Of the three poems recorded at The Cellar, "Statue of Saint Francis" and "Junkman's Obligato" were earlier works put to Lippincott's "free-form jazz," but "Autobiography," his best poetry-and-jazz achievement, "developed right along with The Cellar sessions.... When you do it this way, the poetry reads better as a result."[15] Ferlinghetti is an oral poet, and this strengthens his poetry-and-jazz experiments. Explaining that "The big thing is the oral message. My whole kick has been oral poetry,"[16] he lists as models Vachel Lindsay, Carl Sandburg, and Dylan Thomas, poets who kept their verse true to a spoken form. His ear for slang and contemporary speech as well as his ability to capture an oral stream of consciousness form — man spilling out the beauty and confusion of his mind

— are Ferlinghetti's chief assets. Such a street vitality in speech and a mental associational structure lent themselves to the jazz improvisational form. In "Junkman's Obligato" and "Statue of St. Francis," however, his oral delivery follows speech patterns and do not accommodate the jazz phrasings; hence, speech and thought are captured, but music is not. The chief synthesis that Ferlinghetti achieves is through his intuitively sharp sense of timing. In "Autobiography," however, he adopts a new pattern of a fuguelike alternation between the poetry and jazz. As Ralph J. Gleason explains, "the poet and band trade statements. Ferlinghetti reads a passage and then pauses while the band improvises four bars of jazz on the chords of 'I Got Rhythm.'"[17] This process eliminates any false sense of synthesis and allows each to develop in separate parallel directions. The poem provides the overall form as poet and music move along through a mood of progressive revelation. Not a real synthesis, it is a happy blend of the two media.

The truest union of poetry and jazz appears in Patchen's work — his poetry-jazz. Patchen's materials varied. At first he relied on the earlier poems from *First Will and Testament* which had an oral form and feel. "State of the Nation" and "Do the Dead Know What Time It Is" use barroom speech patterns and a tavern setting to reflect reality. "Lonesome Boy Blues" is a songlike lament readily adaptable to jazz mood and expression. As John Ciardi observes of Patchen's poetry-jazz treatment, "Patchen's poetry is in many ways a natural for jazz accompaniment. Its subject and its tone are close to those of jazz. And most of it is written not metrically, but in phrase groups that adapt naturally to jazz rhythms."[18] Added to the appropriate material and form is Patchen's powerful voice capable of musical sound and timing effects. Ciardi describes Patchen's voice as "casual, almost matter of fact, yet sensitive, resonant, and immediately engaging. A gentle and easy voice, always deeply concerned for the natural rhythms of speech, yet kept exciting by small modulations and by a superb sense of timing."[19] Using his voice as an instrument, Patchen can blend with the music without competing with it. He achieves commanding yet intricate effects with timing, the kind of rhythmic suspensions characteristic of jazz.

Some early reviews of Patchen's poetry-jazz concerts remark on this excellent blend of voice and music: "The phrases and the ideas are so beautifully woven into the jazz texture, so expertly modulated and timed, that it is a veritable revelation to the ear and the mind."[20] James Boyer May, editor of *Trace,* describes it as "Beyond mere harmonies and antiphonies, these performances are remarkable fusions."[21] Even the method of recording the *Kenneth Patchen Reads His Poetry with the Chamber Jazz Sextet* was devoted to an engaging synthesis: "The poems were first taped, then underscored for the accompaniment, and then re-recorded to the nicely mental phrasings and finely woodwindy sound of the Chamber Jazz Sextet."[22] This was but the first phase of Patchen's poetry-jazz achievement.

In 1959 Patchen found himself with new material, a new musical group, and new approaches. The material on his second album, *Kenneth Patchen Reads with Jazz in Canada,* is diverse. A series of four love poems from his earlier works is recorded to a mellow background and titled "Four Song Poems," including some of his best love lyrics for Miriam: "The Everlasting Contenders," "Do I Not Deal with Angels," "The Sea Is Awash With Roses," and "Not Many Kingdoms Left." In another series titled "Four Blues Poems," Patchen uses a Charlie Parker composition to join with his poems: "There's a Place" (titled "Where" in *Hurrah*), "They Won't Let You In There" (titled "It's Because Your Heart Is Pure, Honey" from *When We Were Here Together*), "A Sigh Is Little Altered" (titled "It Is the Hour" from *Hurrah*), and his standard "The Lonesome Boy Blues." Titles as well as lines are altered in the poetry-jazz delivery. Also of note is that Patchen had developed in the selections from *Hurrah* his own poetry-jazz form. Carolyn See points out that this "book of peripheral jazz experiments"[23] is a collection of humorous, almost limerick, pieces to be "read to a jazz riff that was written especially for it and for other humorous poems of the same length and mood."[24] Such poems as "THE CELERY-FLUTE PLAYER" and "I WENT TO THE CITY" from *Hurrah,* which are accompanied by a whimsical drawing, suggest the free improvisational mind controlled only by a time form — a characteristic of jazz. The poetry is influencing the jazz, and the jazz, it seems, is influencing the poetry.

The album's third movement, "As I Opened the Window" is a prose poem selection from *The Famous Boating Party* whose comic and irrational context includes a character-narrator who reveals self and world through his freewheeling speech form. The final movement represents yet another poetry-jazz innovation; "Glory,

Glory'' consists of selected speeches from Patchen's off-Broadway play *Don't Look Now*. White hot with anger at man's world, the play incorporates the jazzman's view of life as well as his vernacular. It is a further synthesis — a jazz-poem-play.

Complementing the adaptation of old material to jazz and the creation of the new jazz-poem forms, Patchen brought a new method of recording poetry-jazz. The Alan Neil Quartet consisting of Alan Neil (piano), Lionel Chambers (bass), Dave Hillary (alto sax), and Bill Boyle (drums) focused the musical composition to a more intimate group, one capable of more and closer interplay with each other. In Alan Neil's description of the session he recalls how ''somebody (Kenneth, I think) hit on the idea of each of us having earphones. We put them on— and we had a scene! It was extremely exciting! Now we could aim our language, our feeling, at Patchen's — the thing had come to life!''[25] Remarkably, words and music and the third variable of vocal delivery are superbly matched. More than matched, they are woven together as all elements truly do listen and respond to each other. Working within the framework of established jazz compositions, the musicians let Patchen's words and delivery guide their own improvisations. Uniquely, Patchen listens closely to the music and responds vocally, as an instrument would, to cultivate pauses, make deliberate holds, execute effective emotional dynamics, and actually slur words into musical phrase patterns. As most jazz singing is a kind of talking of the lyrics, Patchen's poetry recitations are a kind of talking-singing. Like singers Billy Holiday or Ray Charles, Patchen is able to enlarge the emotional expression through the reservoir of pain inherent in his resonant voice.

''Blue Poems'' and ''Poems as Songs'' are moving musical achievements. Unlike Rexroth and Ferlinghetti's treatment, the music begins the pieces and Patchen brings in the words when he feels it. Then all moves along the loose composition form improvising against and with each other. Neil's description of the ''Glory, Glory'' selection made from his arrangement of ''Dixie'' and Patchen's speeches from *Don't Look Now* is revealing. Though full of the jazzman's rhetoric and superlatives, it captures Patchen's power as the group began ''wailing'': ''We had all been caught up in the reading from the start — we knew that something was happening, that this was 'something else' — but now he really went out for it, he wailed! With our nerves, our hearts, we heard him coming on, ringing the changes, threading and pulling us in and out of the light — the King Cat making the scene! And on his face we could see that what we had to say back to him was making the same kind of 'heart-sense'. It was *there*."[26] This is Patchen's "hot" jazz, full of anger and pleading with the world, as he takes off blaring with voice and words as man's lost conscience.

A further improvement Patchen brings to poetry-jazz is the absence of a demanding sense of written logic inherent in the poet's material. He, like the musicians, is free to state whatever he is thinking and feeling without a rigid syntax to follow or a pretense of reasoning to make. Patchen uses his own non-reasoning in all the poems from *Hurrah* and in "As I Opened the Window" where a slightly dazed persona narrates a series of irrational events without causes. The staple jazz elements of humor and irony are characteristic of Patchen's work, as in "Glory, Glory" where a tirade on America's hypocrisies is played ironically against the patriotic refrain of "Dixie." Thus the basic musical compositions provide a context or environment out of which the musician's or the poet's statement acts in counterpoint or reinforcement. Such improvisation within a group of fellow musicians, as any jazz musician knows, places a high demand on honesty. One is immediately judged by his associates. Patchen's personal sincerity and his honest materials and methods of poetry-jazz prove themselves in the authentic and empathetic response of his musicians.[27]

III   *Modern Jazz and Patchen's Poetry Compared*

In conception, both modern jazz and the experimental poetry of Patchen are emotional arts. Both are characterized as anti-art, for as "jazz is debunking the myths of 'fine art' and the social pretensions of the concert hall,"[28] so the avant-garde literature of Patchen and others continually seeks to grow beyond the limits of traditional literary forms. Both, therefore, demand a new and separate set of standards to be judged by. Concerning the contemporary relevance of jazz expression, The Reverend Mr. Alvin L. Kershaw speaks eloquently and simply: "Jazz helps us be sensitive to the whole range of existence. Far from offering us rose-colored glasses ... it realistically speaks of sorrow and pain ... it helps us relate and interpret the variety of experience we have had ... jazz stimulates us to feel deeply and truthfully ... jazz thunders a mighty 'yes' . . . it offers us an urgency to live fully.''[29] This declaration is precisely the overriding functional design of Patchen's art, particularly his poetry-jazz.

Jazz is also conceived, more so than classical music, as extremely dependent on individual expression. Like Patchen's art, it is a form based on the man who makes it, of himself. Not confined but liberated by another man's composition, the jazz musician's only limits are his own conceptions and skills. As Gunther Schuller explains, ''Jazz's strength and communicative power lie in this individuality, which comes from inside the man.''[30] Dedicated to and designed by the individual's free emotional reaction to the world, jazz is man's expressionistic statement of his relationship to the world. Jazzman and Patchen alike capture the pace and psychic state of modern man's mechanical madness. With a keen sense of social absurdity, they can contrapuntally play against it, or they can play an emotional and lyrical statement of the world's wasted beauty. In this way a sense of the world is reflected and answered in their art.

Following from their similar conception, both jazz and Patchen's experimental poetry are closely related in method of creation and in structural forms. Stearns works out a definition of jazz as ''a semi-improvisational American music distinguished by an immediacy of communication, an expressiveness characteristic of the free use of the human voice, and a complex flowing rhythm.''[31] Although virtually all proponents of jazz recognize improvisation as a basic ingredient, they all are quick to point out the depth and control lying behind such improvisation. While Leroy Ostransky describes a type of ''free improvisation'' bearing ''the same relation to jazz that so-called automatic writing does to prose,''[32] he quickly clarifies that this type of creating ''outside the bounds of conscious memory''[33] is not the typical method of jazz improvisation. Rather, ''jazz improvisation consists almost entirely of creating new melodic patterns to 'fit' a given harmonic foundation that . . . usually has a melody of its own.''[34] Though melody is finally abandoned for harmonic variations, the improvisation is based on this prior material. The jazzman improvises, not spur of the moment, but as a result of his past listening, absorbing, and analyzing. He, like the poet practicing free or open or 'field' composition, ''knows that the intangible qualities of imagination, intuition, and inspiration are in part the result of experience and knowledge.''[35] The jazz improvisation is basically a performance of an intuitive, heartfelt response to a jazz composition and to fellow musicians, based on prior training and experience. Trained to respond imaginatively and creatively to established material within a loose basic structure, the jazzman "modifies and adapts, to his individual conception of jazz, melodic fragments, rhythmic patterns, and even entire phrases he has heard and admired."[36] The poetry-jazz improvisations of Patchen fit within the mainstream of jazz; based on his own prior material and that of jazz compositions known to him, he adapts and modifies his own line phrasings to a jazz feel, not a speech feel, and he rewrites some of the wording as he goes.

Much of Patchen's own poetry and anti-novels seem to be based in part on the semi-improvisational method of jazz creation. He always maintains a loose but recognizable form out of which he can respond with intuition and imagination. This method of creation is based on knowledge, skill, and experience, and takes for granted an awareness of forms and a desire to improve on them. Patchen's art, like his poetry-jazz experiments, is basically a performance — at its best a skilled and creative development of form built upon the man and his response to the world. Jonathan Williams records one method of Patchen improvisation in his account of transcribing Patchen's fables:

We established a routine of two or three hours' work, morning and afternoon, with me at the typewriter and Patchen in bed working from occasional scraps of notes, but, primarily, just out of the air. As he would get into a particular fable ... I would read back to him what we had thus far on paper. Then he would proceed, unerringly, to dictate the tales. In some cases the initial typescript served as the basis of rewriting; but often the text emerged directly, fresh from the extraordinary tap Patchen has to his realm of Spirit.[37]

How much and often Patchen relied on this kind of improvisational writing based on fragmented written material and his skill with language, is impossible to say. The *Fables* is a radically imaginative work, yet Williams' account does establish Patchen's familiarity with the semi-improvisational method of creation. Most evident, however, is that the method of jazz creation does much to explain Patchen's own approach and artistic achievement.

A further parallel between Patchen's method of creation and that of the jazzman is their mutual dependence upon a force outside themselves. For Patchen, this force is a mystical belief in wonder; for the jazz musician it is a "jazz spirit" guiding his work. A highly imaginative and "hep" muse speaks to poet and jazzman alike as André Hodier explains, "From an examination of the jazz musicians' own words, it is possible to glean the subtle, unruly, and almost mystical concept of the jazz spirit or feeling, or thinking — it is all of these things and is so understood by the jazz musician himself."[38] Like the jazzman's sense of a force guiding his truest creative impulse, Patchen's faith in the unity and wonder of life give authority to his wildest and truest creative impulse.

Poetry and music have long been compared for their emotional appeal, their subtleties of statement, and their rhythmic and tonal similarities; if we take this comparison to Patchen's open form poetry and to jazz, we find further basic similarities. In the improvisational art of both jazz and open form poetry, many discernible patterns and structures are apparent. Based on a structure of theme and variations, the jazz musician's statements are both basic and unique. The standard twelve bar plan of the Blues and the short transitional pattern of the riff are comparable to open form structures. Timing and transitional patterns are thus built into the open forms of both arts. So much is taken for granted and abbreviated in both jazz and open form poetry that "in-group" awareness has become essential to both.

Tension and release, as Ostransky points out, constitute a basic ingredient of jazz. Like the fist that alternately clenches or extends itself to you, the jazzman's communication is an empathetic experience with his world. Patchen's personal style operates in much the same manner involving us in a continuing struggle with life awareness; it pushes and pulls us, demanding our engaged response. In an emotional self-statement, jazzman and Patchen create an involved form through rhythmic suspensions and/or contrapuntal effect. Patchen's "Do the Dead Know What Time It Is" (1939), as one of his early poetry-jazz works, demonstrates a system of counterpointed thought and dialogue. In a barroom an old man is moved to speak of his life while the young couple he blindly addresses contemplate sex:

> Son, I am going to tell you something
> The like of which nobody ever was told.

(and the girl said, I've got nothing on tonight;
how about you and me going to your place?). (*C.P.* 96)

Such an harmonic system of juxtaposition with ironic effects is the basic structure of many of Patchen's anti-novels as well as his shorter poems and prose. Perhaps the best example of his rhythmic use of jazz suspensions is "Lonesome Boy Blues," another poetry-jazz work. The poem reads as neither speech nor thought, but as a musical blues phrase:

> Oh lonesome's a bad place
> To get crowded into
> With only
> Yourself riding back and forth
>
> On
> A blind white horse. (*C.P.* 419)

Using the slight felt pause at the line's end, he is able to create a subtle blueslike effect as the line flows onward through the pregnant pauses and emotional phrasing. It is thought expressed as feeling, a treatment characteristic of all the poems in *Orchards Thrones & Caravans* (1952) and of much of the phrasing effects of his poetry in general.

Patchen, like the prolific jazz maker, is continually creating individual effects through the free reign of patterned and understood forms. Never confined by form, he uses it, instead, as a means of expanding his own ability to capture and reflect his world. As a pioneer of poetry-and-jazz and a perfector of poetry-jazz, and as a writer who follows parallel paths of conception, creation, and form with jazz, Patchen created an art form enhanced by its relationship to this equally bold and unique American music.

CHAPTER 10

Irrational Tales and Verse

I N the late 1950's Kenneth Patchen's writings underwent a basic
shift in emphasis, one that reflected a similar shift in philosophy.
Increasingly, Patchen turned from an angry protest and unfulfilled
pleading to a firmer commitment to capturing the ever-present
wonder of life. Embracing an innocent and imaginative response to
the daily miracles of the world, Patchen's "wonder" provides subject and form to his final period of writing.

The first work of what might be termed his "wonder period" is
the 1953 prose *Fables and Other Little Tales*. Composed of short,
fantastic, and irrational tales and fables, the book is full of fun,
play, and excitement with life. Though Patchen's more conventional poetry continued into the mid-1950's, followed by his poetry-jazz experiments which further developed his ability to write intuitively, the poetry too turned increasingly to the creation of
wonder. Irrational verse forms evolved with *Hurrah for Anything*
(1957), followed shortly by *Because It Is* (1960). These three collections comprise in prose and poetry the main developments of his
irrational forms. The picture-poem volumes that came later —
Hallelujah Anyway, But Even So, and *Wonderings* — develop further this vein of "wonder" works.

The titles from this period immediately reflect both a conditioned awareness of man's social absurdity and a consequent turning from it. A celebration in the midst of apparent emptiness is
exclaimed. These works, as the poem "WE MEET" indicates, are
"painful rejoicings" (*Hurrah*, 18) performed in open recognition
of man's madness. Rather than an escape into fantasy, they disclose an alternative way of approaching the world through continued belief in the meaning and beauty of Patchen's divinely created
world. Firmly based in his contrasting views of the world of man's
godhood and man's reality, they are built upon the absurd sense of

139

the human condition, the modern contradictions of death in the midst of life, of terror and destruction in the midst of wonder. Truly a poetry of man's absurd, their irrationality comes from their refusal to accept man's conditioned system of reasoning. Like Dostoevsky's underground man in the *Notes*, they are Patchen's own affirmation of the conclusion that "twice two makes five is sometimes a very charming thing too."[1]

Based on an assumption concerning the validity and value of all that social man terms "irrational," these writings serve multiple purposes in Patchen's world vision. First, by contrast they present an alternative world predicated on imagination, intuition, free association, and a reversal of man's logic. As such they serve to point out the inherent and limited assumptions upon which man's sense of logic is based. Man's sense of the rational is exposed for what it is, a single level of consciousness. Second, by introducing and requiring the reader to participate in Patchen's system of irrationality, new alternatives of thinking and perceiving are discovered. He does create a world that commands our attention.

As the cover notes for *Because It Is* accurately proclaim: "So powerful is Patchen's rejection of the world we read about in the newspaper — the supposedly real — that we find ourselves accepting the dictates of his imagination with full belief and following him with mounting excitement — and a sense of joyous release — into a world that *does* exist because of Kenneth Patchen."[2] One becomes engaged in a world, like Tolkein's Hobbit land, where the author's sheer will and fanciful powers validate its existence. Crucial is not what the work says to us but what it *does* to us as reader participants. As any communication requires a modification of self, a bending to speak or to listen to another, so reading Patchen's irrational verse draws the reader into an acceptance of new awarenesses. It requires a new you by the power of its vision. John Holmes describes the process: "The world of Kenneth Patchen is complete in its own fantastic system. Its population, animal, human and otherwise, has never really been counted or described — and would-be census-takers have come back with a dazed sort of shining on their faces and have never been the same since"[3] Rather than escape through art, Patchen creates a form to transform his audience — the functional goal of all his works. Holmes' description of the dazed "would-be census-takers" also warns of the impossibility of a conventional appraisal of this fantastic writing.

However, following our recognition of Patchen's functional design within his world view does reveal the method behind the supposed "madness" of this art. Patchen does devise techniques to create his irrational world.

I *Irrational Art*

Some immediate clarification can be gained by relating Patchen's individual form to other art predicated on a similar design. The cover notes of *Aflame and Afun of Walking Faces* (the revised edition of the *Fables*) suggests this analogy: "To give some notion of the fables, imagine Mark Twain and Leopardi collaborating on a script for the Marx Brothers to act out at the birth of a world — by no means necessarily this one." Identifying ingredients of wit, imagination, and a gift for the bizarre, the analogy also recognizes the art's functional goal of calling for the new "birth of a world." Kenneth Rexroth reveals in his analysis of *Hurrah* that "Patchen has gone back to the world of Edward Lear and interpreted it in terms of the modern sensibility.... It is as if, not a slick *New Yorker* correspondent, but the Owl and the Pussycat were writing up Hiroshima."[4] Likening the form to "free verse limericks" such as Lear might write were he alive today, Rexroth sees Patchen's design as a reaction to and a recording of the world's insanity, all done through the fantastic and incongruous. Patchen's "DON'T TELL ME" from *Hurrah* suggests Rexroth's insights:

> I saw a light up in the sky
> Never knew they smoked cigars up there
> I heard a noise off on the water
> Since when the fishes start packin' guns...
>
> I saw the Clean Man a-standin'
> 'Way up above the world
> And what his eyes were wet from wasn't laughin'.
> (*Hurrah*, 17)

Here images of man's violent world transformation (perhaps Hiroshima) are recorded on an innocent consciousness that notes the obvious wrong in the tears of God. Man's insanity glares against the superior rationality of Patchen's world.

Other revealing comparisons can be made with surrealist and

Dada art. Jonathan Williams, who originally published the *Fables*, simply calls it "American dada."[5] This appraisal both reveals and distorts the work, for whereas both Patchen and the Dadaists sought to transform through irrationality the tenets of philosophy, art, and logic, the Dadaists did so through destruction and nonsense. Patchen's art is based on a belief in wonder as a positive goal, and he is philosophically and aesthetically opposed to the Dadaist methods of violence and destruction. He is more akin to the surrealists, whose belief in the positive value of sur-reality resembles his own faith in wonder. More than ever before Patchen is seeking the surrealist goal of irrational "automatic" creation in art. His earlier surrealist work always presented the problem of his obvious conscious control. As Charles I. Glicksberg notes concerning *Memoirs of a Shy Pornographer*, "It is Surrealism with a difference, mad as any dream, disheveled, lecherous, absurd, fantastic, though always under conscious control."[6] Always reluctant to surrender to the subconscious as the main guiding force in his early work, Patchen increasingly trusts the irrational subconscious forces in this period of wonder writing.

As Jonathan Williams has recorded of Patchen's improvisational and free associative method of writing the *Fables* (see p. 136), the irrational tales and fables required and validated new dimensions for Patchen's subconscious creation. Perhaps loosened by his experiments with poetry-jazz improvisation, Patchen's final period of writing seems the most free and uniquely innovative. Included in this "wonder period" are various syntheses of poetry, prose, jazz, drawings, and paintings — as impulse, intuition, and free association all allow Patchen a fuller realization of the "total artist" role he so diligently seeks. Aware of man's dark reality, Patchen's seemingly irrational creations are emotive projections against the night. In a comic absurd bubble of speech, Patchen's voice is kept going. Instead of passively waiting for a return to wonder, he seeks to create it in his art.

As never before, the irrational tales and verse represent Patchen's achievement of a joint simultaneous form: to reflect and reject madness, to demand personal engagement, and to declare and teach the way of wonder. Where these thematic premises of his vision have been present separately in earlier works, they are now made integrally one, as an awareness of madness demands a personal engagement in the superior reason of unexplainable wonder.

The title premise of *Because It Is* demonstrates this new integration well. Each poem begins with a BECAUSE and follows with an explanation; the explaining, however, is all done in "wonder" logic, which is man's illogic. Exposition is actually the basic motif of all these works, and to understand the explaining one must adopt the premises of the world view. As John Steinbeck writes in *Sea of Cortez,* "To most men the most hateful statement possible is 'A thing is because it is.' Even those who have managed to drop the leading-strings of a Sunday-school deity are still led by the unconscious teleology of their developed trick."[7]

Patchen's irrational works begin with this simple assumption, an acceptance of the miraculous wonder in common things. His explanations are only further exclamations of the simple wonder in it all. To return us to the perspective of the child, we are given the typical child's answer to the unexplained — "Just because!" Patchen would return the magic of the inexplicable and reject a world limited by man's inflated sense of rational analysis. The marvel of living is restored in such poems as

> *BECAUSE* MY HANDS HEAR
> THE FLOWERS THINKING
>
> I scooped up the moon's footprints but
> The ground climbed past with a sky
> And a dove and a bent vapor . . .
>
> O we, too, must learn to live here;
> To use what we are. O fall in now!
> For only love is community! . . .
>
> Our lives are watching us — *but not from earth.* (*Because,* 34)

Title and opening lines defy "rational" explanation, yet communicate both beauty and love in "wonder" logic, where anything is possible. In the context of the irrational, Patchen's reader is thus free to respond to new stimuli. The exposition arrives in the direct affirmation of love, and love comes easily in this environment where men can change the world by simply learning "To use what we are." For Patchen, we are creatures capable of creating a better world by sheer will, but first we must be loosened from our limited reasoning, and that is the intent of his art.

In another poem, *"BECAUSE* ABOVE THE CLOUDS /

LITTLE FROGOOSES FLOATED,'' he begins: ''The Countess
Cherrywhite left her shoeshine stand / And hurried down to
Texas...'' In this irrational context Patchen plays on his theme of
man's insane violence, by allowing the Countess to speak:

> Dey got laws dat say no boy
> What's not in his right mind can
> Molest innocent folks lessen he's provided wit'
> De proper Christian license to snuff dem out
> On a rational, scientific basis... at a million or two
> A clip, by Gar! (*Because*, 52)

In this new perspective, the reasoning which sanctions the mass kill-
ing of innocents by bombs is disclosed as a human absurdity.
Reflecting and parodying societal insanity, Patchen creates a world
where the commitment and engagement are to life and wonder.
    In *Hurrah,* Patchen moves through a series of images and reac-
tions to this man-made world. It is a time:

> When the day seems to die
> In our arms;
> And we have not done
> Much that was beautiful. (*Hurrah,* 25)

This sense of the times captured here in "IT IS THE HOUR" all
leads to the conclusive explanatory poem of this book, "LIKE I
TOLD YOU." Explicitly Patchen expounds his approach to revealing the meaning in wonder by comparing himself with "The Bird of
the Mountain" which:

> Was strolling around
> Making up a little song
> Maybe to the sun
> Or for his special friends
> Or just to himself
> And maybe for no reason
> That anybody could tell you about
> Sort of like I'm doing right now. (*Hurrah,* 62)

The proletarian goal of performing a mass social change has been
transformed into an inward personal engagement with life; Marx

has been traded for Freud and Thoreau. Patchen's "little songs" are the casual poems here dedicated to those like himself who have turned to others whom they can touch personally. The poems need no other authority or "reason" for being than their own inexplicable response, "Just Because!"

The tales and fables of *Aflame and Afun of Walking Faces* share these premises as they too offer both a therapeutic release from logic and a reflective perspective on man's world. Written in a semi-improvised oral form, they are wild hilarious tales of imaginatively real creatures. They act on the mind like the scrawled title Patchen gives to one:

> NO TITLE ON THIS'N
> SMOKEY JES KEP A EATIN
> MOFF FASTAS DYNEMITE PIE. (*Aflame,* 15)

Like "dynemite pie," they are calculated to explode the reader's imagination into new realms of the possible, new ways of thinking and being. In the opening "THE WALKING FACES" he presents the metaphors for our times as "a flood of faces that hurriedly rushes nowhere ... wheels spinning like a pity of hands on an overturned schoolbus. Years and thrones gathered into the crowded nothingness" (*Aflame,* 1). In fantastic images, given an acceptable matter of fact context, Patchen uses a method employed by E. E. Cummings to portray both a sense of life's present emptiness and its murdered innocence, "an overturned schoolbus." The answer to this state is only suggested by the vague faces which might be "the clowns again. Those other saints. Poor thinkamajugs of an all too short eternity" (*Aflame,* 1).

Drawing his own personal and fantastic symbols, Patchen suggests the magic and saintly humor of the clowns as a general balm for the world's ills. The clown is an apt symbol for his irrational writing: traditionally he is set apart from society by his mask and costume; his comic actions defy cause and effect relationships; his rebellion is a triumph of disrespect, and his comic optimism reveals an awareness of absurd reality and a rebellion against it. In the tales that follow, wit, fanciful images, and totally incongruous contexts are used to demand a surrender to Patchen's world. For only by a personal engagement in this world can one participate in its joy. It is the comic-serious fun of clowns which leads us to bend forward wide eyed in anticipation for anything.

The book's closing image presents us with a typical irrational-wonder picture: "And there, people with silver bucketed heads were being tossed back and fortn by two enormous children behind whom, his palely spotted tail covering the sky, a ghost-white rooster stood, negligently pecking at an unseen string of the kind packages of dust are said to come fastened with" (*Aflame,* 84). In Patchen's realm a slavish rationality is seen as a handicap, and only an equally imaginative response can allow the reader admission to his art. Against the image of giant children tossing about empty-headed adults, what the mammoth rooster is loosening can only be projected — atomic fallout or clouds of wonder dust.

These poems and tales are the reader's fanciful lessons in learning to be children again. They require an unlearning of our conditioned way of thinking and a following of Patchen's model of free creation. Like a jazz musician, he is blowing these poems and tales out of his free improvisational mind. They reel out at us defying the objective, rational patterns, and they thus create in us states of mind, states of wonder. Because approach is so crucial, Patchen's art is designed to convey that approach. The medium is made the message by having the form function to instill the state of wonder. This can be demonstrated by a brief examination of Patchen's techniques of the irrational.

II   *Techniques of the Irrational*

The most prominent characteristic of the poems and tales of this period is their refusal to take the rational path. As a technique of irrational creation Patchen uses free association as the loosest kind of structure. His verse takes all the turns that do not go "someplace." Of these associational turnings, Jonathan Williams says, "Never had Patchen's 'go with it' technique, in which one thing does *not* lead to another, made more sense to me."[8] His "AND WITH THE SORROWS OF THIS JOYOUSNESS" creates an expanded state of mind by bringing associational turnings to an alphabetical listing:

> O apple into ant and beard
> Into barn, clock into cake and dust
> Into dog, egg into elephant and fingers

Into fields, geese into gramaphones and hills...

This climaxes in:

> ...vines
> Into villages, webs into wholenesses and years
> Into yieldings .. O zeals of these unspeaking
> And forever unsayable zones! (*Hurrah*, 60)

Here the listing device, another of Patchen's loosest structures, allows an intuitive associational creation. There is also a movement from objects ("apple" and "ant") to abstracts ("wholenesses" and "yieldings"), which depicts in part the path of free association. The result is the happy discovery of the "unsayable zones" of an intuitively free mind. The process makes its own rewards.

In *Aflame and Afun* we see a less obvious application, as he begins:

> HOW THE PROBLEM OF WHAT
> TO HOLD CREAM IN
> WAS EVENTUALLY SOLVED
>
> Once upon a time a lovely little All-Blue-Pitcher
> fell sound asleep in the ram's wool shop. (*Aflame*, 2)

The associative phrasing begins with "Once upon a time a lovely little"; then there is a deliberate free turning to "All-Blue-Pitcher," and again the irrational shift follows as it fell not down, but "asleep in the"; again an unexpected turn takes us to a "ram's-wool shop." Thus Patchen's free mind leads him and the reader to undiscovered zones. A little more extreme and with more comic results, Patchen's "RIGHT NIECE, WRONG UNCLE— / OR VERSA VICE" follows his "go with it" mind to:

> A headlong Spinstress, who had only that sallow, unkempt morning returned after a lank absence to town, changed to stumble on the Mayor in a huddle beside a rosy and plumpish wall; soupon, with perhaps less caution than sagacity, she at once sank her blushing teeth into his most exposed person. (*Aflame,* 10)

The irrational road leads to wildly surprising results and to new

ways of thinking. Notable is the fact that the method of free unreel-
ing association is done with the sentence syntax as the only established structure. This technique is thus an irrational one based on
the inherent possibilities of language. Like his elaborate puns, language forms prompt his free associations.

In other tales and poems, Patchen creates his own words (associatively, of course) within the syntactic pattern of a sentence. An
example of this peculiar technique can be found in:

A MORNING IN BIC-BIC
IN THE GOOD OLD DAYS

Here outside meadow'n moorlet, the goosetooth
Dawn waits by the chipped pink zinc sink;
Waits for Samallyn, who is there, to yearn
Roguishly up the masked trash-treader's funnel.
                                        (*Hurrah,* 38)

Typically, Patchen's created terms are simply an imaginative juxtaposition of two conventional words, very often objects, such as the
"goosetooth" or the "trash-treader's funnel." While the effects of
this device are difficult to define, it obviously leads to humor and
an imaginative treatment of commonplace objects. Yet it also suggests contradiction, for there is a seeming pattern of logic (the syntax), but within it there is actually an illogic (irrational words).
Such a form intimates the contradictions within society, where a
surface pretense of rationality fails quite to cover a chasm of insanity. A further possibility of the form is its demonstration of the
superior order of Patchen's wonder-reason where there is ready
room for the imaginative. Simultaneously, the result is an expanded
view of logic and irrationality.

"THE THREE VISITORS" from *Aflame and Afun* reinforce
this contradictory feeling: "An insouciant little Pelagic Breeze,
finding himself in somewhat elegiacal surroundings with the
declension of night, stealthway penetrated into the shanty of a certain unjocund Cup-fashioner, where, dismayed by the powdery
glabrosity of his host, he began, ebulliently, to cozen some eviticial
catholicon" (*Aflame,* 26). Sentence tone, diction, and pattern are
all quite serious and direct; however, the addition of the inane
nouns creates a comic, even absurd, feeling. Again our false sense

of rationality is parodied and questioned — our instruction in the irrational by example.

Contradiction is also at the heart of *Because It Is*. In "*BECAUSE* HE KEPT IMAGINING A PENSIVE RABBIT" one of the book's recurring crazy creatures, the absurd "little green blackbird," appears in these terms:

> The little green blackbird went off outdoors
> And sat on a tree under a spreading chair.
> When the sun came out it got dark
> But the little green blackbird hadn't ever
> Felt that lonely before and he laughed. (*Because,* 41)

Paralleling so many things in man's world, including man's own sense of himself, "the little green blackbird" is an embodiment of the contemporary contradiction — in the midst of wonder man makes terror and lives in absurd darkness.

Patchen also adopts irrational juxtaposition, seen most commonly in his cataloguing, as an irrational technique. In the above poem, for example, his mind leads to this absurd list:

> So the door closed, the rain closed,
> The sun closed; also, the moon, a jar
> Of raisin pudding, the tenth of January,
> And half a racoon.... (*Because,* 41)

We are thus further trained in adopting an imagination capable of joy and wonder. In "*BECAUSE* THE SMALL MAN / WAS A STRANGER" Patchen's ability with the inherent possibilities of language foster this comic combination of two complementary poems within one. The italicized letters provide the second text:

> On the dark meat of the sky
> Bright dabs of mu*star*d began to appear,
> And a *moo*dy following of *crows* accompanied
> Them to her door. Once safely inside
> The *small m*an banged his head
> On a *beam* and proceeded to fall
> Into a sewing basket on the *couch*. (*Because,* 63)

Particularly comic is the slapstick timing achieved through sam's hitting the *"beam"* and falling into the sewing basket on the *"couch."* Patchen becomes a clown of language. Using his irrational and free associational devices and his comic juxtapositioning, he creates initial kernels for his works from which the absurd conclusions grow.

"THE EVOLUTION OF THE HIPPOPOTAMUS" begins with this grouping: "Once a horse, a gawky countryboy, a striptease queen and an old featherduster decided to set up house together in a sort of windmill which had been newly remodeled to their purpose and specifications" (*Aflame,* 59). One can only begin to imagine what their "purpose and specifications" might be, and this is exactly where the fun lies, in the art of following one's inspired impulse. Structurally, the form is more of a continuous projection that builds from itself rather than a conscious organization from outside. Patchen is generating from the "free mind" as he would have his readers do. Defying rational analysis, his wonder images simply *mean* what they *are.*

A distinct oral feel to the delivery of the irrational tales and verse is conveyed, as though we are all in a room listening to the happy utterances of a dazzling narrator. In fact, Patchen did record many of the poems from *Hurrah* on the poetry-jazz album *Kenneth Patchen Reads with Jazz in Canada,* and there are the early tapes of the *Fables,* which Jonathan Williams mentions, as well as the later recording of *Fables* taped by Kenneth and Miriam Patchen in 1960 and released in 1974. Perhaps performing poetry-jazz influenced this oral delivery or the semi-improvised oral transcription used for *Fables.* The ultimate effect is one of a contagious joy of expression that adds spirit to the poems and a healthy authenticity of an already engaged persona-narrator. The results can be comic and absurd as in "I AM TIMOTHY THE LION" from *Hurrah,* or they can become personally poignant as the narrator turns to direct confrontation with the reader, as in "ALL THE ROARY NIGHT":

> It's dark out, Jack
> The stations out there don't identify themselves
> We're in it raw-blind, like burned rats. (*Hurrah,* 33)

In both moods, an active character narrator speaks directly in lines arranged in conversational phrase patterns.

All of the *Fables* are delivered in the oral story telling style of old, with parenthetic asides and a jocular vibrance of tone. Patchen begins one: "A Hanger-on who had never really succeeded in coming to grips with himself, chanced one evening to notice a streetcar on the ledge just outside his window. Thinking it a scaffolding of some kind, he leaned forward on his careless cigarette-flowered couch and asked the motorman..." (*Aflame*, 19). This intriguing narrator who so nimbly and matter of factly unreels his imagination for us makes the humor of the absurd situation even more appealing. Such oral whimsicality is a general trait of all the works generated in Patchen's wonder period.

Patchen drawings accompanying each poem or tale constitute yet another important technique of the irrational. Although these visual components will be examined more completely in the following section, one must recognize the integral power his drawings have to instill the "free mind" in the reader-viewer. Labeled as "poems-and-drawings" or "fables-and-drawings," the graphic and written forms are mutually interdependent. Like the poem, the expressionist drawing is meant to create states of mind that will lead to wonder. In a kind of absurd expressionism, the drawing reinforces the validity of the imagined world of the writing. In *Aflame and Afun,* for example, Patchen tells the gentle story of "THE DOLT AND THE PRETTY DAMSELS" followed by an equally simple and loving drawing of this extraordinary creature (*Aflame*, 12). Thus a whole realm of fantasy creatures, including a "goofy beduck," "A FIRETREE," a "flybynight" to name a few, are depicted in drawings as a direct rendering of the contents of the writings. At other times, the drawings seem more an abstract and impressionistic response to the tales, as in many of the ink blots and drippings found in *Hurrah.* Large blocks of black, swirls of gray, and sharp thin lines depict vague states of awareness given shape by the corresponding poem in juxtaposition. As in contemporary experimental films, aural and visual are brought together to reinforce each other and to create new expanded states of consciousness.

Based on an intense awareness of society's conditioned and limited view of reality, Patchen's irrational forms and techniques offer an art, not of neurotic escape, but of deliberate commitment to the world possible through an expanded mind. One must begin with himself is his message. Frederick Eckman describes this concept as the broadened base in Patchen's later work: "I note that Patchen's satire, a virtue of the early poems, seems to be absorbing itself into the larger pattern of his mature work; that his rollicking sense of the comic has mellowed into humor; that his intensely personal love lyrics are widening out into a gesture of compassion toward all things created."[9] Particularly in the "wonder period" of his later works one sees a merging adaptation and synthesis of his strongest individual characteristics. Satire and comedy have broadened and deepened into a humor of "absurd" mankind, and a more mellow and resonant commitment has arisen to his world of dynamic wonder.

CHAPTER 11

Painting and Writing Forms

THE writing career of Kenneth Patchen is interwoven with his visual experimentation. Many Patchen books include: self-painted covers, evidence of the printing press used as a painter's brush, drawings printed with poems, or picture-poem posters. Though he never considered himself a "painter," in the one exhibit of his graphics, held at the Corcoran Art Gallery (Washington, D.C.) in 1969, he did allow himself to be called "A Painter of Poems." His visual forms are thus seen as supporting and expanding the written ones. In subsequent posthumous exhibits at Stanford University, the San Francisco Art Institute and the University of North Dakota, Patchen's graphics have included his unique "painted books," paintings, silkscreen folios, handwritten poems, concrete poetry, and his original "picture-poems." All of which reveals that Patchen closely approximated the "total artist" ideal gained from William Blake. As a master creator in multimedia he achieves a developing fusion of the arts of painting and writing, operative within his functional theory of art and his guiding world vision.

Miriam Patchen has accurately charted the growing fusion of painting and writing as a progression from an "understanding" in the "painted books," through an "engagement" in the "drawings and poems," reaching a "marriage" in the total synthesis of the "picture-poem" form.[1] Just as Patchen merged the arts of prose and poetry, of the visual and aural forms in concrete poetry, of jazz and poetry, so his synthesis of painting and poetry further reveals his artistic direction and achievement. By following the progression of this experimental innovation, one arrives at the unity of painting and writing, the culmination of Patchen's art.

153

I   *The Painted Books*

In 1937 Patchen experienced a "violent attack of back disability"[2] which kept him physically confined, but which led him into
the world of graphic arts. By 1942 he had originated the first of his
"painted books," published as *The Dark Kingdom*. In all, there
were to be nine limited editions of "painted books" comprising
over a thousand unique hand painted volumes, all done by Patchen
himself.

His methods and materials for painting these books were as
unique as his images: "Patchen follows a basic procedure in painting these books which begins by adhering special Japanese paper to
the cardboard cover or by painting directly on the bare cardboard
using gouache base. To the prepared surfaces are applied myriad
pigments which include carbon inks, mortar-ground watercolors,
casein, cloth dyes, and the highly favored Japanese earth-colors.
Generally front and back covers are painted and often the back
extends the imagery of the front."[3] Added to this list of materials
are the surprising and unconventional media of coffee, tea, Easter
egg dye, cornstarch, and Japanese sumi sticks and glue. Besides
brushes, Patchen uses such unlikely instruments for application as
tree sprigs, "kitchen utensils, sponges, and a whole range of house-
hold and garden utensils."[4] From this startling array of materials
Patchen created equally fantastic and vibrant book covers for his
limited editions of: *The Dark Kingdom* (1942), *Sleepers Awake*
(1946), *Panels for the Walls of Heaven* (1946), *Red Wine and
Yellow Hair* (1949), *Fables and Other Little Tales* (1953), *The
Famous Boating Party* (1954), *When We Were Here Together*
(1957), *Hurrah for Anything* (1957), and *Poemscapes* (1958).

Patchen's painted books, some of which are pictured in the Corcoran Gallery pamphlet *Kenneth Patchen: Painter of Poems* and
The Argument of Innocence collection, are unique for their personal use of color, their fantastic creatures, and their vibrant and
primal life. Like his writing, they are a strange mixture of simplicity
and imagination. Richard Bowman, an artist and friend of
Patchen's, describes these painted books as "absolutely unique in
their conception; they have the same wry, magnificent and natural
humor that flows from him when he writes."[5] As though made
from wonder itself, their tone is that of comic and joyous beauty
delivered in rich simplicity. Bowman remarks on "the meeting and

happy marriage of apparently dichotomous images, just as in the best Surrealist works. His sense of color, too, is very personal — sometimes extremely subtle, sometimes trenchantly powerful. Just as Patchen creates new forms of poetry, so does he often create some oddly pungent but successful combinations of color and form."[6] Radically experimental and abstract, Patchen's paintings are true to his creative stance as an innovator. His lack of formal training in painting results in an innocent and pure creativity that is both spontaneous and original.

Patchen, however, educated himself in the art of painting, and his tastes and insights are revealing. In an interview Patchen mentions as creative models the painters Van Gogh, Picasso, and Paul Klee. In Van Gogh he admires the courageous innovator, "whose breaking with tradition seems almost as though he didn't know what to do next, and I think this is the stance of the creator."[7] Like Van Gogh, Patchen's paintings employ splashes of color, unconventional application of paint, impressionistic rendering, and, of course, a radical break with tradition.

Patchen admired Picasso equally for his creative stance. Finding Picasso best at an intuitive, spontaneous creativity, which they share, he states: "I feel that in the act of creation there is always a losing of contact with the medium; and when this happens to a marked degree, as happened in the case of someone like Picasso at a certain point, it leads to a breakthrough. In other words, what the artist has no thought of becomes what other artists are full of."[8] As fellow artists, these two innovators share a personally unique and daring style in terms of color, figures, and primal simplicity. Both use analysis and synthesis as creative tools and as a means to engage their audience.

In a third comparison, with Paul Klee, whose work most closely resembles Patchen's own, the description of Klee's creative approach does much to explain Patchen's as well. Patchen explains. "For instance, a man like Paul Klee. I feel that every time he approached a new canvas it was with a feeling that 'well, here I am, I know nothing about painting, let's learn something' — and this is what distinguishes the artist of the first rank, the innovator, the man who destroys, from the man who walks in the footsteps of another."[9] Both Patchen and Klee were destroyers of the bounds that convention and tradition had placed on art and on creators of unexplored forms.

Although comparing one original experimentalist with another usually reveals only basic similarities in approach, in the case of Patchen and Klee it also presents striking parallels. In the art of each, line drawings are used to depict mood and to suggest a narrative; both artists create fantastic figures (surprisingly alike) from a primal imagination, and both use blotches of color to create abstract shapes which serve the expressionist function of instilling mood environment. As daring and innocent creators, both men share a comparable fantastic imagination where primal roots are felt and captured. One could go on to liken Patchen to other artists such as Joan Miro, whose visionary and primal creatures and whose personal color sense resemble his own, or to Jackson Pollock, whose painting decorates the record jacket of Patchen's *Selected Poems* and whose methods are as radical, abstract, and expressionistic as Patchen's; but ultimately the recognition is that Patchen's art is alive, and uniquely his own.

Gene Detro's analysis of Patchen's paintings begins with a recognition of the art's fundamental demand for audience engagement. He finds the paintings: "like dreams, like the world itself — and take a design and meaning from the chemistry of one's own perception. They are original, then in the strongest and most physical sense. Like the universe once a person gets past the illusory field brought on by ego-based seeing. They are firm, real as rocks, purposeful and ultimately open-ended ... the choice being more-or-less between hungup habits of perception and addressing the object (any object) with clear, unafraid, real eyes. Permissive creativity."[10] Patchen's painting shares the creative position of all of his experimental art. It is a demand for engagement and a visual lesson in the perception of wonder through "permissive creativity." Working toward the "total book" ideal of the work done completely by one artist, Patchen suggests and demands through the covers of his "painted books" the new perception required of his world.

II   *Poems and Drawings*

Progressing from an "understanding" of painting and writing in his "painted books," Patchen arrives at an "engagement" relationship between the two media of poetry and drawing in what he terms "poems and drawings." Three volumes in particular contain the deliberate parallel printing of a poem or fable with a drawing by the author. Generated from the same impulse, poem and drawing reinforce, rather than illustrate, each other in their shared expression. *Hurrah for Anything, Because It Is,* and *Aflame and Afun of Walking Faces,* which represent Patchen's irrational tales and verse, also contain this experimental form. Further, two editions of silkscreen folios — *Glory Never Guesses* and *A Surprise for the Bagpipe Player,* which were later printed in bound form as *The Moment* and in the collected bookform as *Wonderings* — contain handwritten "drawings and poems" as well as Patchen's "picture-poems." Unfortunately, however, the brilliant colors are sacrificed in current book reproductions.

In all cases the functional intent of the "poems and drawings" is to create states of mind in the reader-viewer through the shared creativity of the two media. Like the illuminated pages of William Blake, the ancient Celts, or of the Bible, they are intended not merely to 'decorate' but to bring about the light of awareness. A highly intuitive, imaginative, and associational art, Patchen's work is based on the belief that a freely created form will deliver a creative response and will thus free the viewer's mind. This idea is the chief calculation behind the separate and parallel placement of drawing and poem. Such an engaged text demands the audience's working out the relationships of the two forms, a relationship characterized not by logic, but by free and imaginative associations. One must surrender to the wonder of the synthesis and thus be transformed through the very act of perception. In *Hurrah for Anything,* for example, Patchen relies on the irrational or extrarational impressionism of ink blots, swirls of paint, and abstract forms, as well as fantastic creatures and human caricatures to convey moods and attitudes appropriate to the poem. *Because It Is* follows a closer correlation between creature drawings and the narrative of the tale, yet it too uses bizarre means to create fantastic forms.

One critic, Alfred Frankenstein, says of Patchen's creatures: "The only thing consistent about the creatures that inhabit these paintings is that they all have eyes. A good many of them also have beaks and legs and hair, but whether they are birds, people, octopi, or cats is sometimes problematical."[11] Puzzlement is not Patchen's intent, rather the gentle beasts serve to validate and reinforce the marvelous state engendered through the irrational tale or poem. Frankenstein comes closest to recognizing Patchen's functional form when he declares that "the creatures are a facet of the rueful optimism suggested by the book titles."[12] In *Because It Is,* for instance, a comic irrational compounding of nouns generates the new word-creatures. Thus are depicted "the foxy chairabbit and the goffy beduck," a "leafrog," the "flybynight," a "ground creature," "the boy-headed lark" among others, as well as the recurring symbol-motif of the "little green blackbird."[13] At times Patchen will attempt to depict both the creature and the action of the poem in visual form, as in his presentation of "A FIRETREE / SHOOK HANDS WITH ORION," or "MR. FLOWERS THE BOATMAN / SAILED WALLS" or the more tragic and detailed rendering of "THE WHOLE WORLD WAS ON FIRE."[14]

This technique of correlating creatures with tales is consistent throughout Patchen's books of "poems and drawings," as is his reliance on abstract forms and ink blots, drippings, and swirls to capture and instill appropriate mental states. In the silkscreen folios Patchen moves closer to the total integration of picture and word that he later achieves in the "picture-poems" where poem and drawing move from a parallel to a fused form. In the folios, lettering and painting are often interwoven instead of simply juxtaposed. Using handwriting for all the silkscreens, Patchen paints the words as well as the objects. Thus, his "poems and drawings" represent both a formal achievement and a basis for understanding the experimental forms to come.

Due to its extreme reliance upon the response of the viewer, the effect of this method is difficult to gauge. What can be noted, however, is the way form and function are woven into the fabric of the work as the painting shares in the expression and design of the word. Engagement, a state of wonder, and a recognition of man's limited rationality are shared functional goals. Patchen himself helps to clarify the integral approaches used in each mode of expression when he explains: "It happens that very often my writing with a pen is interrupted by my writing with brush — but I think of both as writing. In other words, I don't consider myself to be a painter. I think of myself as someone who has used the medium of painting in an attempt to extend — give an extra dimension to the medium of words."[15] It is the same kind of visual-verbal experience of the world found in poet Robert Bly and artist Wang Hui-Ming's 1972 work *Jumping Out of Bed.*[16] Here the combined arts of poetry and woodcuts extend each other in a joint expression of life's simple wonder.

In the silkscreens, as in all of Patchen's work, there is an underlying suggestion that through innocent imagination, through a recognition of wonder, we are all engendered with a capacity to create art. Indeed, Patchen's narrator of *The Journal of Albion Moonlight* assures us, "I tell you that it is not altogether unreasonable to expect anyone in the world to produce a work of art" (*Albion,* 161). The art testifies not only that wonder exists, but that it is a generative, creative force. Just as Patchen brought the media of jazz and typography to poetry, so he is seeking here to broaden, "to extend," through drawing the expression possible through the word. Thus the truest approach to the fantastic creations of the final "wonder period" in Patchen's art is to view it as an original art form created for the sole purpose of helping man realize — *"BECAUSE* TO REALLY PONDER / ONE NEEDS WONDER" (*Because,* 76).

Because one Patchen creature is *not* like any other, a sample from the work must not be generalized too broadly. However, *Hurrah for Anything* does include what might well be a self-portrait of Kenneth Patchen. In "ONE WHO HOPES," one can see both the philosophy and the form come together. This straightforward poem with its wry and rueful humor is arranged in successive stages of reader-viewer awareness. Below the simplistic portrait of "One Who Hopes" are these lines:

> Born like a veritable living prince
> With small, pink, rectangular feet
> And a disposition to hair, I stand
> Under the blazing moon and wonder
> At the disappearance of all holy things
> From this once so promising world;
> And it does not much displease me
> To be told that at seven tomorrow morning
> An Angel of Justice will appear,
> And that he will clean up people's messes for them —
> Because if he is, and he does, he'll be more apt
> To rub their lousy snouts in it. (*Hurrah,* 34)

One meets first the gentle smiling creature in drawing and description, then progresses through the poem to the realization that the hope is not only for wonder, but also for Justice — to clean up man's insanity and "To rub their lousy snouts in it." Ideally, through identification, one also realizes that we are part of both the wonder and the madness. We detect in the drawing's facial expression a look of innocence and marvel. This rough yet basic shape is like a figure from our childhood suggestive of the ready wonder in the essential and spontaneous. It is what one brings to the drawing, however, that renders it complete, as the simple lines for face and body animate the bold black sphere. On completing the poem, we return to the face which now seems to haunt in a shadowy forewarning. This is the message and promise Patchen would bring, and he does it here through the happy combination of the poem and the drawing.

III *Picture-Poems*

The "picture-poem" of Patchen's final period of productivity represents an ultimate synthesis of painting and poem and a culminating achievement of his ideals of the "total artist" and the "total book." His last three books *But Even So, Hallelujah Anyway,* and *Wonderings* are handwritten (devoid of print or page numbers) and totally designed and executed by the master craftsman who has become a "painter of poems." In the "picture-poems," painting and poem, visual and verbal, have been merged, not merely juxtaposed for illustrative value, but as one unified form and expression. The poem has moved from outside the drawing, as in the "poems and drawings," to within the painting as a "picture-poem" form. The catalogue of Patchen's Washington, D.C. exhibit defines and describes them as: "Not to be confused with illuminated manuscripts which usually isolate the word and image, Patchen's picture-poems achieve an ineffable bond of the verbal and visual. While retaining the integrity of both verse and picture, the fusion of the two creates an extraordinarily affective form of poetry. Any Patchen picture-poem allows for experiences which are both aural and visual."[17]

Sharing the intent of the "poems and drawings," the painting and poem are combined in an effort to extend the expression of each. As Milton Klonsky describes it, "The poems cum pictures by Kenneth Patchen ... are not 'illustrated' poetry, but rather the poems themselves extended into the modality of the visible."[18]

Visual shapes, creatures, colors, and designs are, as it were, welded in space with the personal presence of the handwritten poems. More than sharing the page, word and painting combine in the creation of a new form. Like the true synthesis of two media in poetry-jazz, so here Patchen has achieved the "marriage" of two related media in his own original form.

The bulk of this work was produced during the last ten years of Patchen's life when physical confinement had brought him to accept painting and writing as his only means of creation. In the bedroom of his Palo Alto cottage, the paint brush was as close as the pen, and he began to use both together. His friend Norman Thomas describes Patchen's bedroom studio: "If you visit Patchen at midmorning . . . the sun will be spreading out, diffused, across tables bright with opened pots of paint and tufted with fists of paint brushes, over piles of books and sheets of painted poems, coming to rest as stripes on a tousled yellow and orange bedspread."[19] In this small space Patchen learned to extend through his art his world and ours.

Two earlier works forecast the development of the "picture-poem." *Cloth of the Tempest* (1943) contains twenty-one pages on which Patchen drew both form and handwritten poem. All are in black and white; many border on concrete poetry; many use a collage of printing, another artist's drawing, and Patchen's hand-written poem. The best, however, are of Patchen's own simplistic sketches of a room or a creature combined with a short, integrated and boldly written poem. Most of these unified works have been included in Patchen's selection of the *Collected Poems*.[20] Many of the panels of *Panels for the Walls of Heaven* (1946) combine drawing or painting with a verbal message, often a one word statement as in "War" and "Sleep,"[21] and occasionally a painting alone. He also uses the recurring statement "god understands but forgives" lettered over the painted panels of six different forms. Color and paint are used in *Panels* as well as ink drawing, and the combined effect is much like the epigrammatic works of many of the later "picture-poems."

Hallelujah Anyway (1966) is Patchen's first volume of "picture-poems," including eighty-three of the forms, many of which had appeared earlier as *Patchen Cards,* a collection of gift art-cards.[22] *But Even So* (1968) contains forty-five "picture-poems," originally printed on yellow paper, and each introduced by a facing page stating the title theme. *Wonderings* (1971), Patchen's last original work, contains the thirty-six poems from the earlier silkscreen folios as well as additional paintings, handwritten poems, and picture-poems.

Setting a precedent for the "poster art" of contemporary pop art, Patchen's work is unified by the power of his world vision with the wonder of his individual imagination. Some revealing comparisons to his visual-verbal art form are found in the works of artists Paul Reps, Ben Shahn, Stuart Davis, and Joan Miro. Reps has worked out picture-poem combinations closely resembling the Chinese art of the ideogram, where word and object are approximated.[23] This was also a preoccupation of the earlier Imagist poets who sought to capture the unity of object, form, and word. Ben Shahn has transformed his early training in lithography into an art which combines typography, hand lettering, and vibrant painting. In addition to textual illuminations, he has worked with Chinese characters and Hebraic lettering, and he has also used a clever integration of verbal message and visual design to sound a social protest, as in the "Stop H-Bomb Tests" painting of 1960.

Stuart Davis also shares Patchen's and Shahn's vision of a socially responsive art. An important force in the Pop Art Movement, Davis long worked at combining letter and word forms with abstract expressionism of line forms. Joan Miro also explored the common grounds of painting and poem in what Alain Jouffroy terms "Picto-poetry."[24] Miro's work with illustrating the works of other writers such as Tristan Tzara, René Char, and Alain Jouffroy, ultimately led to *Le lézard aux plumes d'or,* his own picture-poem book. All these artists have established the combination of two media into one art form as part of the creative process. Milton Klonsky's recent study places Patchen in the development "of the picture poem from Geoffry Whitney's sixteenth century emblem poetry to e.e. cummings, Kenneth Patchen and the concrete poets."[25]

Such an engaged art requires an equal imaginative and spontaneous response from its audience. One must respond emotionally and aesthetically to the visual form while working out the new relationship of visual form and verbal messages. As Alfred Frankenstein observes, there is a unity of design to be comprehended in Patchen's picture-poems: "Most of the time Patchen's text, painting, and lettering join in a unity demonstrating beyond a shadow of a doubt that the whole is greater than the sum of its parts.''[26] As always, Patchen's keen sense of function in form seeks expansion through synthesis. Medium and message unite as the artistic experience presents and requires a living experience of wonder.

Gene Detro asserts of the fusion of statement and engaged action found in Patchen's picture-poems: "Patchen's paintings say: Wake up! Join me in making! ... If you don't know you work in partnership with God in creating the world every day — if you don't know you don't have to be afraid of me — well, that ain't my fault, pal. Thus do they render a service — like dreams — at the roots of a viewer's being."[27] This is Patchen's personalism of style and design projecting itself through the visually engaging art. A fusion of wonder and engagement achieved in the picture-poems comes as a sense of recognition. It is an *experience* and can only be suggested here through a few selected models.

In "GLORY NEVER GUESSES," the title poem from his 1955 silkscreen folio, one detects a growing correlation between visual and verbal forms. Here the poem is strategically written within the picture frame; title and painting are in matching gray ink, and the smooth flow of the lettering done in dark curves suggests individuality and care. A paralleling of plot between poem and painting occurs in the depiction of the cycling "Smiling Moose" and the heart shaped "forgetmenots." Much like a valentine in its visual presence, this picture-poem brings two additional qualities to the traditional celebration of love. There is the comic absurdism of the moose and of the blushing beaver enhanced by the nonsense lines "With a rupple-dupple-dobbie-o / With a sneggle-keggle-owego," but more emphatic is the awareness brought in the final lines to reality. "Love's worth all the sad," he assures us and thus acknowledges an experience with the dark night of civilization. The poem stands strengthened by its mature affirmation of love in the face of societal emptiness. (The picture-poem can be found in *Wonderings.)*

Patchen's handwriting adds much here to complete the picture-poem. It is strikingly uncharacteristic of the other handwritings, which are usually etchy, wobbly, written or printed in varying shades — for Patchen seems to have as many lettering styles as poems. This piece offers a tone of assuredness and individual beauty, rising to the emphasis of the concluding couplet in a slightly larger and bolder sweep. His commitment to love remains as strong as his demand for imaginative wonder, and though there is a heavy reliance on the written medium here, theme and form are one in this early model of the picture-poem.

Another characteristic of Patchen's picture-poems is the implicit cosmological statement which occurs in all the works of the final "wonder period." In this model from *Hallelujah Anyway* Patchen presents a dualistic analogy in a dualistic form. Abstract figures and concepts reinforce each other on the facing page

LOVE (WHICH INCLUDES POETRY), *Hallelujah Anyway,* 1966.

Diagramed we have these relationships:

LOVE (poetry)   ⎯ > ⎯ SCIENCE
CHILD CATCHINGS ‖ ⎯ > ⎯ ‖ HANGMAN'S THROES

The words printed in various shades and sizes accent the positives of LOVE, POETRY, FREE & BEAUTIFUL, CHILD, whereas SCIENCE and HANGMAN are printed in contrasting thinness which makes them appear diminutive. Such wording seems to "happen" on the page in an appropriate relationship to the abstract figures. Lettering goes right around and up into the abstract forms, molding it all together as one radiating expression. One is tempted to define the graphic objects, which have only an eye and legs in common, as the imaginative "CATCHINGS" of childlike amazement. In elemental reduction, poem and picture suggest the simplicity and assurance of wonder, and thereby signify a rejection of man's insanity.

The concluding picture-poem from *But Even So* symbolizes the progression toward simplicity and summing up, characteristic of Patchen's final writings. Creating his own iconography, Patchen reduces his language to the verbal conciseness of Confucian or Zen proverbs. In "ALL THAT LEAVES," he uses a patterned yet individual background (Many of Patchen's picture-poems are projected against a wallpaperlike design of his own drawing.) and achieves a balanced distribution of elemental and tripartite figures which are interwoven with individual handwriting. The words read slowly and resonantly due to their broad form and distribution, as all life is summed up in this seeming paradox: "All That Leaves / Is Here Always."[29] The iconography suggests that the egg (upper left) and the sperm (lower right) are united by the central creature's fetal

LOVE (WHICH INCLUDES POETRY), *Hallelujah Anyway*, 1966.

suggestion. The classic myth of "the chicken and the egg" is also implied by the upper left figure of an egg enclosed hen — a western parallel to a Zen riddle.

What Patchen is affirming in such primal simplicity is the unity of life principle basic to his vision. The *one* and the *all* are emphasized as they partake of the life design that includes all as part of each other. James Boyer May finds such reconciliation to be an inherent element of Patchen's picture-poems: "For, he writes and paints with certain abstract understanding of the reconcilement of ego with what Jung called the anima; through his work, he consciously activates the encompassing *Ego* which is both larger *Self* and selfless. His best things are acts of reunion."[30] In this primal quality of Patchen's art one feels an elemental contact with a visual and verbal archetype. Like his characteristic of giving eyes to all things (even the sperm possesses a single eye in *But Even So*), his philosophy sees the life principle residing in all animals, objects, and ideas. This is his answer to a world that man finds devoid of meaning; it is an affirmation of life as a growing and eternal process. Out of its presence comes the wonder which creates itself in Patchen's free and love centered life. His art ultimately becomes his summation of life.

CHAPTER 12

Conclusions

I N his "Elegy on the Death of Kenneth Patchen," Lawrence Ferlinghetti presents the existential position of the artist's life work:

> A poet is born
> A poet dies
> And all that lies between
> is us
> and the world.[1]

The poet, his life, his audience, and his world — these are the essential elements that must be grasped in any attempt to deal with Kenneth Patchen's art. As a symbol of the unity he espoused, his life and art are one. They partake of that unity of existence where one recognizes that "Any who live stand in one place together."[2]

Shaped by the suffering, the beauty, and the absurdity which he witnessed, Patchen's writing has always been in and of this world. His engaged concern for this world and its blind creature-man provide the overriding function of his art and of his life. Assuming the role of poet-prophet, Patchen would, like William Blake, be the insistent conscience of mankind, standing as a symbolic refusal to accept the limited vision of man's conditioned existence. His art is forged in the furnace of his life vision and shaped into a tool for building. With a requisite function of saving man from himself, the form which the art takes is as strong and practical as Patchen's own will.

Listed within Patchen's own writings are his various artistic models and influences. From a broad spectrum of world literature, they include: Homer, Dante, Shakespeare, Blake, Dostoevski, Heine, as well as the bold and experimental figures of American lit-

166

erature — Herman Melville, Stephen Crane, Walt Whitman, and Hart Crane. He was also deeply affected by radical innovators in painting, political thought, and jazz music. Patchen's own influence on contemporary literature should finally be recognized as the embodiment of the committed artist, for he makes a way for the artist of engagement, for the anti-cool, compassionate creator committed to life in an absurd time. Ferlinghetti accurately portrays Patchen as an exemplar of the socially engaged and idealistic artist:

> . . . he spoke much of love
> and never lived by 'silence exile & cunning'
> and was a loud conscientious objector to
> the deaths we daily give each other.[3]

The passion and will of Patchen's radically new art demand both involvement and new aesthetic criteria. As Harvey Breit early recognized, Patchen's art represents a new challenge to poet, critic, and audience for a life-engaged response.[4] From such personal commitment comes an art naturally integral with its creator, molded to his image as a man. This individuality is a chief characteristic of Patchen's art, and any appreciation of his work must begin there. Harold Norse regards Patchen as "probably the most independent poet of his generation, independent in every sense — a pioneer in style, in subject, in sound, in language, in his special climate of compassionate awareness, in his poetic attitude."[5] Such personal uniqueness of methods and approach makes group classification of Patchen's work meaningless and artificial. He is not revealed but distorted by classification, something he fought against all his life. James Boyer May, critic and friend of Patchen, defines his individuality as one which "cannot be described or in any degree be identified by nationality, station in life, family, or by considerations of political or religious affiliation. . . . This is what makes him the rare sort of person who is capable of thinking and acting primarily through self-awareness and self-containment — able to project unique feelings concerning a world which is, in the philosophical sense, really his own."[6] Thus through an open understanding of Patchen's world do we come to the only true understanding of his art.

Kenneth Patchen's vision of the world is the unifying principle of this study. We have observed his world view characterized by its simplicity, its consistency, and its tripartite structure. Its basis is revealed as 1) a recognition and rejection of "man's madness," 2) a necessary "engagement" in love brotherhood, and belief, and 3) a sanctioning of "wonder," an innocent, free, and imaginative response to the world's beauty, as the ideal approach to life. In an art which includes joint ideals of the "total book" and the "total artist," Patchen creates engaged forms to realize his view of life. In a continuing struggle against a too narrow definition of art, he devises such radically new forms as the anti-novel in *The Journal of Albion Moonlight* and *Memoirs of a Shy Pornographer,* the startling prose-poems of *Poemscapes* and *Panels for the Walls of Heaven,* the pioneering concrete poetry of *Sleepers Awake* and *Panels,* the contemporary art form of poetry-jazz, the art of irrational tales and verse, and the continued open form poetry. His culminating synthesis in art forms is the result of a progressive development of the painted books, poems and drawings, and finally the picture-poems of his wonder period.

Patchen's art, always predicated on the principle of a passionate engagement in life, reflects the author's visionary progression from a belief in the social conversion of man's madness in the late 1930's and 1940's to a final and total commitment to personal development through wonder, evident in the late 1950's and 1960's of his writing. Patchen is now gaining recognition as a molding force in the development of a radical human consciousness. His art is at one with that world. It is dedicated, as David Meltzer points out, to forcing his audience not merely to recognize but to actually experience an engagement in his world: "Patchen would not have us merely believe in love, man & truth. He would have us *know,* to consider all that is possible within us & outside of us."[7] From his fervent dedication to the unity of life which he found in the world Patchen creates art that gives authority and validity to a life of love, brotherhood, and wonder — the possibilities of this world.

John William Corrington has spoken of the need to approach Patchen through the broad perspective of his total works. He argues convincingly for a Patchen canon: "Strangely enough, Patchen's genius (like that of Faulkner, I think) is not resident in any single work. I cannot name a poem and say, 'this is Patchen's essence.' . . . Possibly this is because, like Faulkner, Patchen knows too much, and no single poem — possibly no single talent — can

make much of a dent in the enormity of such inner experience."[8]
As Patchen's wife Miriam continues to propagate his art and as
publishers James Laughlin and Lawrence Ferlinghetti continue to
make his writing accessible, the Patchen canon of books, recordings, and paintings becomes more of a living reality. Original paths
which he made into art remain for scholarly illumination. Miriam
Patchen now speaks of opening new ways into the man and his art
through writing a biography. Corrington speaks truly: "We need
Patchen. We need his strength and his genius; we need to have his
poetry read and re-read, bought and digested by thousands of
punks and greybeards who have never experienced this man, have
missed a portion of exciting verbal champagne that should be
counted among their cultural inheritances."[9]

Long extolled by his fellow artists and by our 'underground' literary world which has produced such comparable contemporaries
as Richard Brautigan and Kurt Vonnegut, Jr., Patchen has recently
been gaining the broader attention and recognition which he
deserves. He will always have his detractors, but as the importance
of his social message and his aesthetic innovations is more fully
realized, his reputation and readership will blossom. As a visionary
artist of the twentieth century, as a poet-prophet to the contemporary world, Patchen creates an art dedicated to no less than the
salvation and expansion of our world. His artistic achievement
within these magnificent life goals makes his work of permanent
value to us all.

Notes and References

Chapter One

1. Recent anthologies including Patchen's work are: Chad Walsh, ed., *Today's Poets: American and British Since the 1930's* (New York, 1964 and 1972 rev.); Stephen Berg and Robert Mezey, eds., *Naked Poetry: Recent American Poetry in Open Forms* (New York, 1969); Miller Williams, ed., *Contemporary Poetry in America* (New York, 1973); Michael Benedikt, ed., *The Prose Poem: An International Anthology* (New York, 1976).

2. William Everson, from "Homage to Kenneth Patchen," *The Outsider* 2, No. 4/5 (1968–1969), p. 117. The editors have neglected to paginate this section of the magazine. I follow the natural pagination.

3. David Meltzer, "Kenneth Patchen," *Contemporary Poets of the English Language,* eds. Rosalie Murphy and James Vinson (New York, 1970), pp. 839–940.

4. Allen Ginsberg, from "Homage to Kenneth Patchen," *Outsider,* p. 99.

5. Jess Ritter, "Minstrels' Memorial: Shreds of Patchen," *the village voice,* 9 March 1972, p. 21.

6. Richard Hack, "Memorial Reading for Kenneth Patchen at City Lights Poets Theatre, San Francisco: 2 February 1972," *Chicago Review,* 24 (1972), p. 80.

7. Hack, pp. 65–80.

8. Kenneth Patchen, quoted in "Rare Interview with the Poet," by Doublas Dibble, *The Weekender, Alameda Times-Star,* 26 September 1967, p. 6.

9. Kenneth Patchen, *Collected Poems of Kenneth Patchen* (New York, 1968), p. 281. All future references to this book, designated as *C.P.,* will be given in parenthesis in the text.

10. Stanley Kunitz, et al., eds., *Twentieth Century Authors* (New York, 1942), p. 1081.

11. Kenneth Patchen, quoted in *Twentieth Century Authors,* p. 1081.

12. Personal interview with Mrs. Alice McKibben, Niles, Ohio, 20 June 1974.

13. Kenneth Patchen, "Patchen Interviewed by Gene Detro," from "Homage to Kenneth Patchen," *Outsider,* p. 117.

14. Kenneth Patchen, *Hallelujah Anyway* (New York, 1966), #30–31.

Lacking pagination, I have numbered the pages beginning with the first picture-poem.

15. Miriam Patchen, "Biographical Sketch," *Kenneth Patchen: Painter of Poems* (Washington D.C., 1969), p. 6.

16. Miriam Patchen, quoted in an interview "Miriam Patchen Recalls Kenneth," with Susan Berman.

17. Miriam Patchen, "Recalls Kenneth."

18. Kenneth Patchen, "Bury Them in God," *New Directions 1939* (Norfolk, 1939) rpt. in *In Quest of Candlelighters* (New York, 1972), pp. 89–107.

19. Patchen, "Bury Them," p. 102.

20. Patchen, "Bury Them," p. 102.

21. Peter Veres and Miriam Patchen, "Kenneth Patchen: His Life" in *The Argument of Innocence* (Oakland, Calif., 1976), p. 92.

22. Kenneth Patchen, quoted in Henry Miller, *Patchen: Man of Anger and Light,* in *Stand Still Like a Hummingbird: Collected Essays* (New York, 1967), p. 29.

23. Miriam Patchen, "Biographical Sketch," p.6.

24. Harold Norse, from "Homage to Kenneth Patchen," *Outsider,* p. 105.

25. James Laughlin, quoted in Linda Kuehl, "Talk with James Laughlin: New and Old Directions," *New York Times Book Review,* 25 February 1973, p. 47.

26. Anais Nin, *The Diary of Anais Nin, 1939–1944,* Vol. 3 (New York: Harcourt Brace Jovanovich, Inc. 1969) pp. 30–32.

27. Jonathan Williams, "How Fables Tapped Along Sunken Corridors," *Aflame and Afun of Walking Faces* (New York, 1970), p.85.

28. Jonathan Williams, p. 86.

29. Lafe Young, from "Homage to Kenneth Patchen," *Outsider,* pp. 130–131.

30. Ginsberg,p. 98.

31. Miriam Patchen, "Biographical Sketch," p. 6.

32. Doublas Dibble, "Rare Interview with the Poet," p. 6.

33. Dibble, "Rare Interview," p. 4.

34. Miriam Patchen, personal correspondence, 15 February 1974.

35. Miriam Patchen, "Biographical Sketch," p. 6.

36. Kenneth Patchen, quoted in "Rare Interview," p. 4.

37. Norman Thomas, from"Homage to Kenneth Patchen," *Outsider,* p. 96.

38. James Boyer May, from "Homage to Kenneth Patchen," *Outsider,* p. 102.

39. Morton Marcus, quoted in Susan Margolis, "A Reading for Kenneth Patchen," *Rolling Stone,* March 1972.

40. May, p. 102.

Chapter Two

1. Raymond J. Nelson, "American Mysticism: The Example of Kenneth Patchen," Diss. Stanford 1970, p.84.

2. Kenneth Patchen, *Memoirs of a Shy Pornographer* (New York, 1945), p. 98. All future references to this book, designated as *Memoirs,* will be given in parentheses in the text.

3. Kenneth Patchen, *Sleepers Awake,* 2nd ed. (1946; rpt. New York, 1969), p. 291. All future references to this book, designated as *Sleepers,* will be given in parentheses in the text.

4. Kenneth Rexroth, "Kenneth Patchen, Naturalist of the Public Nightmare," *Bird in the Bush: Obvious Essays* (New York, 1959), p. 100.

5. Jonathan Williams, "How Fables," p.87.

6. Amos N. Wilder, *The Spiritual Aspects of the New Poetry* (New York, 1940), p. 181.

7. Charles I. Glicksberg, "Proletarian Poetry in the United States," *Fantasy,* 10, No. 26 (1942), p. 29.

8. Henry Miller, *Patchen: Man of Anger and Light,* in *Stand Still Like a Hummingbird: Collected Essays* (New York, 1967).

9. Charles I. Glicksberg, "The World of Kenneth Patchen," *Arizona Quarterly,* 7 (1951), p. 266.

10. Kenneth Patchen, quoted in "Alan Neil's Account of the Session," *Kenneth Patchen Reads with Jazz in Canada* (New York, 1959), p. 3.

11. Nelson, "American Mysticism."

12. Frederick Eckman, "The Comic Apocalypse of Kenneth Patchen," *Poetry,* 92 (1958), pp. 389–392. William Carlos Williams, "A Counsel of Madness," *Fantasy,* 10, No. 26 (1942), pp. 102–107.

13. Rexroth, "Naturalist," pp. 94–105.

14. Harvey Breit, "Kenneth Patchen and the Critical Blind Alley," *Fantasy,* 6, No. 4 (1940), pp. 21–25.

15. William Carlos Williams, "A Counsel," p. 103.

16. James Dickey, "Kenneth Patchen," *Babel to Byzantium* (New York, 1968), p. 71.

17. Breit, p. 25.

18. Kenneth Patchen, *The Journal of Albion Moonlight* (1941; rpt. New York, 1961), p. 206. All future references to this book, designated as *Albion,* will be given in parentheses in the text.

19. Kenneth Patchen, "Blake," introduction to *The Book of Job* by William Blake (New York, 1947).

20. Kenneth Patchen, "A Letter to God," in *Doubleheader* (1946; rpt. New York, 1965), p. 47.

21. Glicksberg, "The World," p. 268.

22. Miller, p. 36.

23. Patchen, quoted in Miller, p. 30.

24. Kenneth Patchen, "O quietly the SUN-MAN sits," *Wonderings* (New York, 1971), #45; unpaged.

25. Patchen, quoted in Miller, p. 30.

26. Kenneth Patchen, *See You in the Morning* (New York, 1947), p. 155.

27. Miller, p. 30.

28. Kenneth Patchen, "A Note on 'The Hunted City,'" *First Will and Testament* (Norfolk,Conn., 1939), pp. 167–168. Reprinted in *Naked Poetry: Recent Poetry in Open Forms,* eds. Steven Berg and Robert Mezey (New York, 1969), p. 69.

29. John Dryden, quoted in Patchen, "A Note," *First,* p. 168.

30. Glicksberg, "The World," p. 265.

31. Glicksberg, "The World," p. 275.

32. Miller, p. 31.

33. Patchen, "A Note," *First,* p. 167.

34. Kenneth Patchen, quoted in Rexroth, p. 100.

35. Kenneth Patchen, *They Keep Riding Down All the Time* (New York, 1946), reprinted in *In Quest of Candlelighters,* p. 124.

Chapter Three

1. William Carlos Williams, "A Counsel," p. 103.

2. Rexroth, "Naturalist," p. 103.

3. Patchen, quoted in Miller, p. 31.

4. Glicksberg, "Proletarian Poet," p. 29.

5. Rexroth, "Naturalist," p.104.

6. Patchen, *Memoirs,* p. 163.

7. Miller, p. 31.

8. Kenneth Patchen, "A Word," *An Astonished Eye Looks Out of the Air* (Walport, Oregon, 1945), preface.

9. Patchen, *An Astonished Eye,* preface.

10. Alex Comfort, "Introduction to an English Edition of Kenneth Patchen's Poems, 1946," reprinted in *Selected Poems of Kenneth Patchen* (New York: Folkways Records, 1959), p. 1.

11. Kenneth Patchen, *Because It Is* (New York, 1961), p. 38.

Chapter Four

1. Breit, p. 23.

2. Kenneth Patchen, quoted in Detro, "Interviewed," p. 117.

3. Patchen, *Sleepers,* p. 68.

4. Patchen, *Hallelujah Anyway, #3*; unpaged.

5. Patchen, *Wonderings, #2*; unpaged.

6. *Wonderings, #55.*

7. *Wonderings, #87.*

8. Glicksberg, "Proletarian Poet," p. 30.

9. R. Hack, p. 77.

10. *Hallelujah,* #4.

11. E. E. Cummings, "#38," *Poems 1923–1954* (New York, 1954), p. 378.

12. William Carlos Williams, "A Counsel," p. 103.

13. Miller, p. 31.

14. Comfort, "Introduction," p. 1.

15. Nelson, "American Mysticism," p. 168.

16. Nelson, p. 147.

17. Wayne C. Booth, "Variations in Distance," *The Rhetoric of Fiction* (Chicago, 1961), pp. 155–159.

18. Patchen, "Blake," introduction.

19. Patchen, quoted in Detro, "Interviewed," p. 121.

20. Miller, p. 29.

21. Glicksberg, "The World," p. 265.

22. Rexroth, "Naturalist," p. 104.

23. Patchen, "A Note," *First,* p. 107.

24. Peter Veres, p. 26.

25. Nahma Sandrow, *Surrealism: Theater, Arts, Ideas* (New York, 1972), p. 25.

26. Sandrow, p. 22.

27. Patchen, quoted in Wilder, *Spiritual Aspects,* p. 186.

28. James Boyer May, from "Homage to Kenneth Patchen," *Outsider,* p. 99.

29. May, p. 101.

30. Patchen, "A Note," *First,* p. 168.

31. Patchen, quoted in Miller, pp. 29–30.

32. Sandrow, p. 80.

Chapter Five

1. Patchen, quoted in Detro, "Interviewed," p. 121.

2. Patchen, quoted in Detro, "Interviewed," p. 126.

3. See Tony Tanner, *The Reign of Wonder: Naivety and Reality in American Literature* (New York, 1967), for a revealing discussion of "wonder" as an essential element of the Romantic vision in American literature. Suggested as a means of "beholding" the universe and its underlying unity of all life, "wonder" emerges from its European roots in Rosseau, Wordsworth, and Coleridge into the American Transcendental writing of Emerson, Thoreau, and Bronson Alcott. It is part of the underlying idealism of Realists Twain and James and of the essential Romanticism of such moderns as Hemingway, Sherwood Anderson, Stein, and such contemporaries as Salinger and Bellow.

4. Hack, p. 76.

5. Kenneth Patchen, *Poemscapes* (1958; rpt. New York, 1965) in *Doubleheader,* #168; unpaged, but numbered.

6 *Poemscapes,* #118.

7. Patchen, "Blake," introduction.

8. Patchen, "Blake," introduction.

9. Patchen, quoted in Detro, "Interviewed," p. 121.

10. *Poemscapes,* #86.

11. Walt Whitman, "Miracles," *Leaves of Grass,* eds. Sculley Bradley and Harold W. Blodgett (New York, 1973), critical edition, p. 388.

12. Whitman, *Leaves of Grass,* Sec. 31, p. 59.

13. Patchen, *Hallelujah Anyway,* #16.

14. *Poemscapes,* #80.

15. *Poemscapes,* #146.

16. Patchen, *Because It Is,* p. 72.

17. E. E. Cummings, *100 Selected Poems* (New York, 1959), p. 73.

18. Cummings, *100 Selected Poems,* p. 102.

19. Robert Duncan, "Pages from a Notebook," *The New American Poetry* (New York, 1960), p. 404.

20. William Blake, "The Voice of the Ancient Bard," *Songs of Innocence* (New York, 1971), p. 41.

21. E. E. Cummings, "Introduction," *Collected Poems: E.E. Cummings* (New York, 1963), n.p.

22. Lawrence Ferlingthetti, "I Am Waiting," *A Coney Island of the Mind* (New York, 1958), p. 53.

23. Patchen, quoted in Thomas, from "Homage to Kenneth Patchen," *Outsider,* p. 96.

24. Patchen, *Hallelujah,* #79.

Chapter Six

1. Patchen, "Bury Them in God," *In Quest,* pp. 99–102.

2. "Bury Them," p. 107.

3. Kenneth Patchen, "The Journal of Albion Moonlight," (advance flier for *The Journal of Albion Moonlight*).

4. Rexroth, "Naturalist," pp. 102–103.

5. Rexroth, "Naturalist," p. 103.

6. Kenneth Patchen, *They Keep Riding Down All the Time* (New York, 1946) and *Panels for the Walls of Heaven* (Berkeley, 1946), reprinted in *In Quest of Candlelighters* (New York, 1965).

7. Kenneth Patchen, "A Letter to God," in *Patchen: Man of Anger and Light* by Henry Miller (New York, 1946), rpt. in *Doubleheader* (New York, 1965).

8. "A Letter to God," *Doubleheader,* p. 55.

9. *They Keep Riding Down, In Quest,* p. 124.

10. *They Keep Riding Down, In Quest,* p. 126.

11. *In Quest,* back cover.

12. "A Letter to God," *Doubleheader,* p. 49.

13. Patchen, *See You in the Morning,* cover page.

14. Kenneth Patchen, *Aflame and Afun of Walking Faces,* revised edition of *Fables* (1953), (New York, 1970). All future references to this book, designated as *Aflame,* will be given in parentheses in the text.

15. Ezra Pound, "Canto LIII," *Selected Poems* (New York, 1957), p. 147.

16. Philip Stevick, "Introduction," *Anti-Story* (New York, 1971), p. xiii.

17. Stevick, p. xxii.

18. Stevick, pp. v–vii.

19. Stevick, p. .

20. Patchen, "The Journal of Albion Moonlight," flier, n.d.

21. Hack, "Memorial Reading," p. 76.

22. William Carlos Williams, "A Counsel," p. 105.

23. Patchen, "A Note," *First,* p. 167.

24. Stevick, p. xix.

25. Stevick, p. xxi.

26. Anais Nin, *The Diary of Anais Nin, 1939–1944,* Vol. Three (New York, 1969), p. 63.

27. William Carlos Williams, "A Counsel," p. 104.

28. Ibid.

29. Nelson, "American Mysticism," pp. 157–158.

30. Patchen provides internal tables of contents to novels and indirectly to *The Journal of Albion Moonlight* on the following pages: 282–283, 290–295, 300, 301, 302, 304.

31. Nin, p. 64.

32. Kenneth Patchen, *Hurrah for Anything,* rpt. in *Doubleheader* (New York, 1965), p. 26. All further references to this book will be given in parentheses in the text.

33. See p. 104, this book for reprint copy.

34. William Carlos Williams, "A Counsel," p. 104.

35. Ibid.

Chapter Seven

1. *Kenneth Patchen: Painter of Poems,* p. 12.

2. Patchen, *Panels for the Walls, In Quest,* p. 64.

3. Patchen recorded the following poems from *The Famous Boating Party:* "Not Many Kingdoms Left" and "Opening the Window" (titled "As I Opened the Window"), *Kenneth Patchen Reads with Jazz in*

Canada; "Soon It Will" and "In Order To," *Selected Poems of Kenneth Patchen,* both recorded for Folkways Records, New York, 1959.

4. John Peale Bishop, *Nation,* 2 December 1939, p. 620.

5. Jonathan Williams, cover notes, *Poemscapes* (Highlands, North Carolina, 1958).

6. Frederick Eckman, "The Comic Apocalypse," p. 391.

7. Patchen, *Poemscapes,* in *Doubleheader,* #XXIV; no pagination, but numbered. Further references given in parentheses in the text.

8. Eckman, "The Comic Apocalypse," p. 391.

9. Jonathan Williams, covernotes, *Poemscapes* (1958).

10. Patchen, "A Note," *First,* p. 167.

11. Patchen, "A Note," *First,* p. 168.

12. Jonathan Williams, covernotes, *Poemscapes* (1958).

Chapter Eight

1. Hans Arp, "On Concrete Art," in *The Modern Tradition,* eds. Richard Ellmann and Charles Feidelson, Jr. (New York, 1965), p. 53.

2. Mary Ellen Solt, ed., "A World Look at Concrete Poetry," in *Concrete Poetry: A World View* (Bloomington, Indiana, 1970), p. 7.

3. Solt, p. 7.

4. *Kenneth Patchen: Painter of Poems,* p. 48.

5. Solt, p. 8.

6. Solt, p. 13.

7. Solt, pp. 47–51.

8. Jonathan Williams, "The Crooked Cake of Leo Cesspooch; Or How I Survived Bucolic Plague & Came Unto Concrete," in Solt, p. 86.

9. Max Bense, "Concrete Poetry," in Solt, p. 74.

10. Augusto de Campos, et al., "Pilot Plan for Concrete Poetry," in Solt, p. 72.

11. Solt, p. 59.

12. Emmett Williams, ed., "Foreword and Acknowledgements," in *An Anthology of Concrete Poetry* (New York, 1967), p. vi.

13. Solt, p. 13.

14. Eugen Gomringer, "From Line to Composition," in Solt, p. 67.

15. Claus Bremer, in Williams, *Anthology,* no pagination; authors are listed alphabetically.

16. Pierre Garnier, in Solt, pp. 32–33.

17. Claus Bremer, in Williams, *Anthology,* no pagination.

18. Pierre Garnier, in Williams, *Anthology,* no pagination.

19. Patchen, *Panels,In Quest,* p. 53.

20. *Panels,* p. 58.

21. Eugen Gomringer, "From Line," in Solt, p. 67.

22. Max Bense, "Concrete Poetry," in Solt, p.73.

23. For a descriptive cataloguing of Patchen's concrete poetry, see my dissertation "The World of Kenneth Patchen: Form and Function in His Experimental Art,"Diss. Kent State Univ. 1974, pp. 152–155.

Chapter Nine

1. Kenneth Rexroth, "Some Thoughts on Jazz as Music, as Revolt, as Mystique," *Bird in the Bush,* pp. 19–41.
2. "Kenneth Rexroth," in *The San Francisco Poets,* ed. David Meltzer (New York, 1971), p. 23.
3. *Poetry Reading in "The Cellar"* (San Francisco: Fantasy Records, 1957), cover notes.
4. Carolyn See, "The Jazz Musician as Patchen's Hero," *Arizona Quarterly,* 17 (Summer 1961), p. 137.
5. Jonathan Williams, "How Fables," pp. 86–87.
6. A. Neil, *Jazz in Canada,* p. 2.
7. Some sense of constituency and chronology of the Poetry-and-Jazz Movement can be gained from the recordings and their cover notes, as well as *The San Francisco Poets,* pp. 9–55; "The Cool,Cool Bards," *Time,* 2 December 1957, p. 71; Kenneth Patchen pamphlets and ephemera, Kent State University Library, special collections.
8. Carolyn See, p. 138.
9. Kenneth Patchen, "Pomes Pennyeach 1959" (Kent State Univ. Library, special collection of Patchen ephemera).
10. Kenneth Koch, "Biographical Notes," *The New American Poetry,* ed. Donald M. Allen (New York, 1960), p. 440.
11. "The Cool, Cool Bards," p. 71.
12. *Poetry Reading in "The Cellar,"* cover notes.
13. Carolyn See, p. 139.
14. Bruce Lippincott, quoted in *Poetry Reading in "The Cellar,"* cover notes.
15. Lawrence Ferlinghetti, quoted in *Poetry Reading in "The Cellar,"* cover notes.
16. Ibid.
17. Gleason, quoted in *Poetry Reading in "The Cellar,"* cover notes.
18. John Ciardi, "Kenneth Patchen: Poetry, and Poetry with Jazz," *Saturday Review,* 43 (May 14, 1960), p. 57.
19. Ciardi, p. 57.
20. "Pomes Pennyeach 1959," excerpted from *Los Angeles Examiner,* n.p.
21. "Pomes Pennyeach 1959," excerpted from James Boyer May, *Trace,* n.p.
22. Ciardi, p. 57.
23. Carolyn See, p. 142.

24. Carolyn See, p. 142.

25. Alan Neil, p. 1.

26. Alan Neil, p. 1.

27. For a study of Patchen's relationship to jazz saxophonist Charlie Parker, see my dissertation, "The World of Kenneth Patchen," Kent State University, 1974, pp. 174–177.

28. Marshall W. Stearns, *The Story of Jazz* (New York, 1956), p. 282.

29. Alvin L. Kershaw, quoted in Stearns, p. 304.

30. Gunther Schuller, *Early Jazz: Its Roots and Musical Development* (New York, 1968), p. 57.

31. Stearns, p. 282.

32. Leroy Ostransky, *The Anatomy of Jazz* (Seattle, 1960), p. 48.

33. Ostransky, p. 49.

34. Ostransky, p. 63.

35. Ostransky, p. 84.

36. Ostransky, p. 69.

37. Jonathan Williams, "How Fables," p. 86.

38. André Hodier, quoted in Ostransky, p. 26.

Chapter Ten

1. Fyodor Dostoevsky, *Notes from Underground,* in *Existentialism from Dostoevsky to Sartre,* ed. Walter Kaufmann (Cleveland, 1956), p. 78.

2. Patchen, *Because It Is,* cover notes. Further references given in parentheses in the text.

3. John Holmes, quoted in Patchen, *Aflame and Afun,* cover notes.

4. Rexroth, "Naturalist," p.64.

5. Jonathan Williams, "How Fables," p. 87.

6. Glicksberg, "The World," p. 271.

7. John Steinbeck, *Log from the Sea of Cortez* (New York, 1951), p. 86.

8. Jonathan Williams, "How Fables," p. 87.

9. Frederick Eckman, "The Comic Apocalypse," p. 391.

Chapter Eleven

1. Miriam Patchen, "Biographical Sketch," p. 6.

2. Miriam Patchen, "Biographical Sketch," p. 6.

3. *Painter of Poems,* p. 39.

4. *Painter of Poems,* p. 47.

5. Richard Bowman, "Notes from a Friend," *Kenneth Patchen: Painter of Poems,* p. 8.

6. Bowman, p. 8.

7. Kenneth Patchen, quoted in Detro, "Interviewed," p. 119.

8. Patchen, quoted in Detro, "Interviewed," pp. 119–120.

9. Patchen, quoted in Detro, "Interviewed," p. 120.

10. Gene Detro, "Screens Revealing Yourself," *The Weekender, Alameda Times-Star,* 16 September 1967, p. 8.

11. Alfred Frankenstein, "Patchen's Search for a 'Beautiful World,'" *San Francisco Examiner and Chronicle,* 28 January 1973, p. 38.

12. Frankenstein, p. 38.

13. Patchen, *Because It Is.* Pictures and poems of these creatures appear on the following pages: 9–10, 12–13, 20–21, 30–31, 32–33.

14. *Because It Is,* pp. 26–27, 64–65, 66–67.

15. Patchen, quoted in Detro, "Interviewed," p. 119.

16. *Jumping Out of Bed,* poems by Robert Bly and woodcuts by Wang Hui-Ming (Barre, Mass., 1973).

17. *Painter of Poems,* p. 44.

18. Milton Klonsky, *Speaking Pictures: A Gallery of Pictorial Poetry from the Sixteenth Century to the Present* (New York, 1975), p. 212.

19. Norman Thomas, from "Homage to Kenneth Patchen," *Outsider,* p. 96.

20. The picture poems selected by Patchen from *Cloth of the Tempest* may be found in *Collected Poems:* pp. 254, 259, 269, 285, 287, 301, 305.

21. Patchen, *Panels, In Quest,* pp. 28, 36.

22. Kenneth Patchen, *Patchen Cards* (San Francisco).

23. Paul Reps, *Zen Telegrams: Seventy-Nine Picture Poems* (Rutland, Vermont, 1959): *Gold and Fish Signatures* (Rutland, Vermont, 1968).

24. Alain Jouffroy, "Le lezard aux plumes d'or, Poems in Signs, Images and Words," in *Homage to Joan Miro,* ed. G. Di San Lazzaro (New York, 1972), p. 129.

25. Klonsky, cover notes.

26. Frankenstein, p. 39.

27. Detro, "Screens," *Weekender,* p. 8.

28. "GLORY NEVER GUESSES," *Glory Never Guesses and Other Pages* (1955), rpt. *Wonderings* (New York, 1971), no pagination — eighty-third page after dedication.

29. "All That Leaves," *But Even So* (New York, 1968), last page in this unpaged volume.

30. James Boyer May, from "Homage to Kenneth Patchen," *Outsider,* p. 10.

Chapter Twelve

1. Lawrence Ferlinghetti, "An Elegy on the Death of Kenneth Patchen," *Open Eye, Open Heart* (New York, 1973), p. 37. This poem was first read at the City Lights Poets Theatre Kenneth Patchen Memorial

Reading, Feb. 2, 1972, in San Francisco.

2. Patchen, "Any Who Live," *Wonderings,* no pagination.

3. Ferlinghetti, "An Elegy," p. 37.

4. Breit, "Kenneth Patchen and the Critical Blind Alley," pp. 21–25.

5. Harold Norse, from "Homage to Kenneth Patchen," *Outsider,* p. 105.

6. James Boyer May, from "Homage to Kenneth Patchen," *Outsider, p. 105.*

7. David Meltzer, from "Homage to Kenneth Patchen," *Outsider,* p. 129.

8. John William Corrington, from "Homage to Kenneth Patchen," *Outsider,* p. 114.

9. Corrington, p. 115.

Selected Bibliography

PRIMARY SOURCES

1. The Writings.

Aflame and Afun of Walking Faces. New York: New Directions, 1970. Revised edition of *Fables and Other Little Tales.* Karlsruhe, Jonathan Williams, 1953.

An Astonished Eye Looks Out of the Air. Walport, Oregon: United Press, 1945.

Because It Is. New York: New Directions, 1960.

Before the Brave. New York: Random House, 1936. Reprinted New York: Haskell House, 1974.

"Blake," introduction to *The Book of Job* by William Blake, New York: United, 1947.

"Bury Them in God," *New Directions 1939.* New York: New Directions, 1939. Reprinted in *In Quest of Candlelighters.* New York: New Directions, 1972.

But Even So. New York: New Directions, 1968.

"City Wears a Slouch Hat," Radio script. Columbia Workshop, 1942.

Cloth of the Tempest. New York: Harper and Brothers, 1943. Revised edition, New York: Padell, 1948.

Collected Poems of Kenneth Patchen. New York: New Directions, 1968.

The Dark Kingdom. New York: Ganis and Harris, 1942.

"Don't Look Now," Drama. Produced at New York's Living Theatre, 1959; Palo Alto, 1959.

Doubleheader. New York: New Directions, 1965. Reprint of *Poemscapes,* "A Letter to God," and *Hurrah for Anything.*

Fables and Other Little Tales. Karlsruhe: Jonathan Williams, 1953.

The Famous Boating Party and Other Poems in Prose. New York: New Directions, 1953.

First Will and Testament. Norfolk: New Directions, 1939.

Glory Never Guesses. San Francisco: privately printed, 1955.

Hallelujah Anyway. New York: New Directions, 1966.

Hurrah for Anything. Highlands, North Carolina: Jonathan Williams, 1957. Reprinted in *Doubleheader.* New York: New Directions, 1965.

In Quest of Candlelighters. New York: New Directions, 1972. Reprint of

Panels for the Walls of Heaven, They Keep Riding Down All the Time, "Bury Them in God"; also prints "Angel Carver Blues."

The Journal of Albion Moonlight. Privately published, 1941. Reprinted New York: United Book Guild, 1944; New York: Padell, 1945; New York: New Directions, 1961.

Kenneth Patchen ephemera. Kent State University, Special Collections Library, Kent, Ohio. Includes "Pomes Pennyeach 1959," "The Journal of Albion Moonlight" advertisement, poetry-and-jazz concert advertisements and reviews.

"A Letter to God" from Henry Miller. *Patchen: Man of Anger and Light.* New York: Padell, 1946. Reprinted in *Doubleheader.* New York: New Directions, 1965.

The Love Poems of Kenneth Patchen. San Francisco: City Lights, 1960.

Memoirs of a Shy Pornographer. New York: New Directions, 1945, 1965; San Francisco: City Lights, 1958.

Orchards, Thrones and Caravans. San Francisco: The Print Workshop, 1952.

Outlaw of the Lowest Planet. London: Grey Walls Press, 1946.

Panels for the Walls of Heaven. San Francisco: Bern Porter, 1947. Reprinted in *In Quest of Candlelighters.* New York: New Directions, 1972.

Patchen's Lost Plays. ("The City Wears a Slouch Hat" and "Don't Look Now") Santa Barbara, Calif.: Capra Press, 1977.

Pictures of Life and Death. New York: Padell, 1947.

Poems of Humor and Protest. San Francisco: City Lights, 1960.

Poemscapes. Highlands, North Carolina: Jonathan Williams, 1957. Reprinted in *Doubleheader.* New York: New Directions, 1965.

Red Wine and Yellow Hair. New York: New Directions, 1949.

See You in the Morning. New York: Padell, 1948.

Selected Poems. New York: New Directions, 1946. Revised editions: 1958, 1964.

Sleepers Awake. New York: Padell, 1946. Revised edition, New York: New Directions, 1969.

A Surprise for the Bagpipe Player. San Francisco: privately printed, 1956.

Teeth of the Lion. Norfolk: Conn., 1942.

Tell You That I Love You. Hallmark, 1970.

There's Love All Day. Hallmark, 1970.

They Keep Riding Down All the Time. New York: Padell, 1946.

To Say If You Love Someone. Prairie City, Illinois: Decker Press, 1949.

When We Were Here Together. New York: New Directions, 1957.

Wonderings. New York: New Directions, 1971.

2. Long-playing Records of Patchen Reading His Works.

Fables. Palo Alto, California: Green Tree Records, 1974.

Kenneth Patchen Reads His Love Poems. No. FL9719. New York: Folkways Records, 1961.
Kenneth Patchen Reads His Poetry with the Chamber Jazz Sextet No. 3004. New York: Cadence Records, 1958.
Kenneth Patchen Reads with Jazz in Canada No. FL9718. New York: Folkways Records, 1959.
Patchen Reads from Albion Moonlight. New York: Folkways Records, 1974. Recorded 1958.
Selected Poems of Kenneth Patchen No. 9717. New York: Folkways Records, 1960.

SECONDARY SOURCES

Suffering from the critical bias of an avant-garde versus academia dispute, Patchen criticism is, at best, scattered, sparse, and just beginning to form. Listed below are the best critical works on Patchen as well as certain writings which indirectly reveal his achievement. The clearest avenue to an illumination of Patchen's writings remains those articles and chapters by his associates. Among them, of particular merit are the writings of Henry Miller, Harvey Breit, Kenneth Rexroth, Frederick Eckman, Charles I. Glicksberg, and William Carlos Williams most of which are now available in Richard G. Morgan's book *Kenneth Patchen: A Collection of Essays.* To this can be added the recent scholarly dissertations of Raymond J. Nelson and myself. The Corcoran Gallery pamphlet, *Kenneth Patchen: Painter of Poems,* and Peter Veres's collection of Patchen art in *The Argument of Innocence* suggest insights to and examples of his graphics. Richard G. Morgan's scholarly *Kenneth Patchen: A Comprehensive Bibliography* has made us aware of special collections of Patchen material in Kent State University, the Patchen manuscripts in The Kenneth Patchen Archive in Special Collections at the University of California at Santa Cruz, and the collections of letters at the University of California at Los Angeles, the University of Chicago, and Northwestern University. For an excellent pictorial and written collection of Patchen reminiscences by his associates one must consult "Homage to Kenneth Patchen" edited by Jon and Louise Webb in *The Outsider.* (Note that authors in this collection will be listed under WEBB.)

ALLEN, DONALD M., ed. *The New American Poetry.* New York: Grove, 1960. One of the best collections of contemporary American poetry, including poets' statements on their writing.

BENEDIKT, MICHAEL, ed. *The Prose Poem: An International Anthology.* New York: Dell, 1976. Contains representative Patchen pieces as well as a discussion in the "Introduction" of Patchen's interjection of humor into the prose poem.

BERG, STEPHEN, and ROBERT MEZEY, eds. *Naked Poetry: Recent American Poetry in Open Forms*. New York: Bobbs and Merrill, 1969. This contemporary collection includes Patchen's work and his important statement "A Note on 'The Hunted City'."

BREIT HARVEY. "Kenneth Patchen and the Critical Blind Alley," Fantasy, 6 (1940), 21-25. Excellent understanding of Patchen's personal and independent artistic role.

CIARDI, JOHN. "Kenneth Patchen: Poetry, and Poetry with Jazz," *Saturday Review*, 14 May 1960, p. 57. A short review of Patchen recordings as well as a performance of poetry-jazz.

COMFORT, ALEX. "Introduction to an English Edition of Kenneth Patchen's Poems, 1946," *Selected Poems of Kenneth Patchen*. New York: Folkways Records, 1959, cover notes. An interesting and revealing perspective of the radical thrust of Patchen's works.

"Cool, Cool Bards," *Time*, 2 December 1957, p. 71. An early report on the poetry-and-jazz phenomenon.

DETRO, GENE, et al., eds. "A Bay Area Poet's Fight Against Pain," *The Weekender, Alameda Times-Star*, 16 September 1967, 1-12. A special edition devoted to Patchen including reproductions of Patchen's works and critical insights by Detro, Raymond Nelson, and an interview by a Doublas Dibble.

―――――. *Patchen: The Last Interview*. Santa Barbara, Calif.: Capra Press, 1976. A final glimpse of Patchen the man and the artist.

DEUTSCH, BABETTE. "A Poet of the Steel Works." *Herald Tribune Books*, 15 March 1936. One of the earliest appraisals of Patchen as a proletarian poet.

DICKEY, JAMES. "Kenneth Patchen," *Babel to Byzantium*. New York: Farrar, Straus and Giroux, 1968, pp. 71-72. Dickey mixes praise and scorn for Patchen's poetic nature yet lack of form.

ECKMAN, FREDERICK. "The Comic Apocalypse of Kenneth Patchen," *Poetry* 92 (1958), 389-392. Makes a strong case for Patchen's Blakean affinity, and through analyses of *Selected Poems, When We Were Here Together*, and *Poemscapes* suggests the developmental scope of Patchen's poetry.

FERLINGHETTI, LAWRENCE. "An Elegy on the Death of Kenneth Patchen," *Open Eye, Open Heart*. New York: New Directions, 1973. A poetic elegy on Patchen as man and artist.

FRANKENSTEIN, ALFRED. "Patchen's Search for a 'Beautiful World,'" *San Francisco Examiner and Chronicle*, 28 January 1973, 38-39. An analysis of Patchen's graphic works.

GASCOYNE, DAVID. "Introducing Kenneth Patchen," in *Outlaw of the Lowest Planet*. London: Grey Walls Press, 1946. An interesting appraisal from the British avant-garde perspective of the first third of Patchen's career.

GLICKSBERG, CHARLES I. "Proletarian Poetry in the United States," *Fantasy,* 10 (1942), 29-31. An early assessment of the proletarian themes of Patchen's first works.

———. "The World of Kenneth Patchen," *Arizona Quarterly,* 7 (1951) 263-275. A good midpoint assessment of Patchen's career. Plagued by Glicksberg's desire to classify Patchen as a failed Surrealist, the study presents a favorable review from the 1950's.

HACK, RICHARD. "Memorial Reading from Kenneth Patchen at City Lights Poets Theater, San Francisco: 2 February 1972," *Chicago Review,* 24, No. 2 (1972), 65-80. Besides providing the best account of the memorial reading, Hack attempts an analysis of *The Journal of Albion Moonlight* and presents a young contemporary summation of Patchen.

HALL, JAMES T. "Patchen's Angry Shoes." *Poetry,* November 1949. Examines the protest theme in Patchen's writing.

Kenneth Patchen: Painter of Poems. Washington, D.C.: The Corcoran Gallery of Art, 1969. This pamphlet describes and demonstrates Patchen's graphics. An excellent account of his methods and materials as well as a catalogue of his works and biographical and critical selections by MIRIAM PATCHEN and RICHARD BOWMAN.

KLONSKY, MILTON, ed. *Speaking Pictures: A Gallery of Pictorial Poetry from the Sixteenth Century to the Present.* New York: Harmony Books, 1975. Includes samples of Patchen's works and places him in the pictorial poetry tradition.

MELTZER, DAVID, ed. *The San Francisco Poets.* New York: Ballantine Books, 1971. An excellent source for the San Francisco Renaissance. Through a series of interviews of six West Coast poets, Meltzer reveals the cultural atmosphere and chronicles the events. Patchen is mentioned in interviews with Rexroth, Everson, Ferlinghetti, Welch.

———. "Kenneth Patchen," *Contemporary Poets in the English Language,* eds. Rosalie Murphy and James Vinson. New York: St. Martin's Press, 1970, 838-840. A short bio-critical statement.

MILLER, HENRY. *Patchen: Man of Anger and Light,* in *Stand Still Like a Hummingbird: Collected Essays.* New York: New Directions, 1967, pp. 27-37. Though heavily slanted with personal impressionism and an avant-garde defiance, Miller's work was the first (1946) substantial study of Patchen treating both the international character of his art and its dualistic split between protest and compassion. Includes Patchen comments.

MORGAN, RICHARD G. *Kenneth Patchen: A Collection of Essays.* New York: AMS Press, 1977. An excellent collection of the scattered criticism of Patchen. Includes a "Foreword by Miriam Patchen and essays by Breit, Ciardi, Hack, Miller, Rexroth, See, Wilder, Neil, J. Wlliams. W.C. Williams, Glicksberg, and others. Richard Morgan provides an "Introduction."

————. *Kenneth Patchen: A Comprehensive Bibliography.* New York: Paul Appel, 1978. When this study appears it will contain a comprehensive, annotated, descriptive bibliography of primary and secondary works as well as a detailed inventory of all manuscripts and correspondences in public collections.

————. *Patchen's The Journal of Albion Moonlight: Its Form and Meaning.* Albuquerque, New Mexico: Black Cat Books, 1976. One of the few close studies of this important Patchen book.

NEIL, ALAN. "Alan Neil's Account of the Session," *Kenneth Patchen Reads with Jazz in Canada.* New York: Folkways Records, 1959, cover notes. Neil's personal account of Patchen and their poetry-jazz recording in Vancouver, Canada. 1959.

NELSON, RAYMOND J. "American Mysticism: The Example of Kenneth Patchen," unpubl. dissertation, Stanford Univ., 1970. Nelson provides one of the first scholarly treatments of Patchen's works. Associating Patchen with the Whitmanesque strain in American Literature, he attempts to define Patchen's art by correlating it with the mystical path.

NIN, ANAIS. *The Diary of Anais Nin, 1939-1944,* Volume 3. New York: Harcourt Brace Jovanovich, Inc., 1969. Biographical portrait of Patchen in New York days, as well as an impressionistic analysis of *Albion Moonlight.*

NYREN, DOROTHY, ed. *A Library of Literary Criticism: Modern American Literature.* 3rd edition.New York: Frederick Ungar Publishing Co., 1960, pp. 374-377. This collection of critical fragments presents well the critics' dispute over Patchen's art.

PATCHEN, MIRIAM. "Biographical Sketch," in *Kenneth Patchen: Painter of Poems, p. 6.* Patchen's wife gives her perspective on their life and career.

————. "Foreword," *The Argument of Innocence: A Selection from the Arts of Kenneth Patchen* by Peter Veres. Oakland Calif.: Scrimshaw Press, 1976. In addition to the foreword, Miriam Patchen provides a biographical chronology and an interview with Peter Veres. Interesting insights to Patchen's graphic methods and final years in Palo Alto.

REXROTH, KENNETH, and LAWRENCE FERLINGHETTI. *Poetry Reading in "The Cellar,"* with cover notes by Ralph J. Gleason. San Francisco: Fantasy Records, 1957. The cover notes provide an analysis and a chronicling of the poetry-and-jazz event of this recording.

————. "Kenneth Patchen, Naturalist of the Public Nightmare," in *Bird in the Bush: Obvious Essays.* New York: New Directions, 1959. pp. 94-105. Though Rexroth digresses to an avant-garde versus academia dispute, this study remains one of the best introductions to Patchen's art. Particularly revealing is Rexroth's understanding of Patchen's place in world literature and the methodology behind his "madness."

————. "Some Thoughts on Jazz as Music, as Revolt, as Mystique," in *Bird in the Bush: Obvious Essays,* pp. 19–41. Rexroth's explanation of the American Jazz Movement.

RITTER, JESS. "Minstrels' Memorial: Shreds of Patchen," *the village voice,* 9 March 1972, 20–22. His account of the Memorial Reading of February 2, 1972.

SANDROW, NAHMA. *Surrealism: Theatre, Arts, Ideas.* New York: Harper and Row, 1972. An excellent overview of Surrealism with direct parallels to Patchen's art apparent.

SCHEVILL, JAMES. "Kenneth Patchen: The Search for Wonder and Joy." *American Poetry Review,* Jan.-Feb. 1976. A contemporary appraisal which acknowledges Patchen's "Wonder Period" as central to his final works.

SEE, CAROLYN. "The Jazz Musician as Patchen's Hero," *Arizona Quarterly,* 17 (1961), 136–146. Contains a brief discussion of Patchen's poetry-jazz form as well as an analysis of the general influence of jazz on Patchen's art.

SMITH, LARRY R. "The Poetry-and-Jazz Movement of the United States," *Itinerary 7,* Fall 1977, 000. An overview of the Poetry-and-Jazz Movement with particular attention to Patchen's paramount position in its development.

————. "The World of Kenneth Patchen: Form and Function in His Experimental Art," unpubl. dissertation, Kent State Univ., 1974. A scholarly treatment of his art based on his vision of life.

SOLT, MARY ELLEN, ed. *Concrete Poetry: A World View.* Bloomington, Indiana: Indiana University Press, 1970. Though it only obliquely mentions Patchen, this remains the best introduction to and collection of concrete poetry. Parallels in theory and form to Patchen's concrete poetry are apparent.

STEVICK, PHILIP. "Introduction" to *Anti-Story.* New York: Free Press, 1971. Excellent discussion of anti-story and anti-novel forms offers indirect insights into Patchen's experimental prose.

TANNER, TONY. *The Reign of Wonder, Naivety and Reality in American Literature.* New York: Harper and Row, 1967. See this excellent study for an understanding of the American literary tradition on "wonder." Its applications to Patchen's vision are apparent.

Tribute to Kenneth Patchen. (anon. ed.) London: Enitharmon, 1977. This collection of poem and prose tributes to Kenneth Patchen contains contributions by William Everson, Lawrence Ferlinghetti, Howard Schoenfeld, Charles Wrey Gardiner, James Schevill, Diane di Prima, Bernard Kops, Michael Horovitz, Joel Climenhaga, Hugo Manning, Lars Gustav Hellstrom, Jonathan Clark, and Diane Wald. Distribution is by Berkeley, California: Serendipity Books.

VERES, PETER. *The Argument of Innocence: A Selection from the Arts of Kenneth Patchen.* Oakland, Calif.: Scrimshaw Press, 1976. Includes excellent color reproductions of Patchen's graphics — concrete poems, painted books, drawings-and-poems, picture-poems, and miniature sculpture. Also presents an interview with Miriam Patchen and a biographical chronology.

WALSH, CHAD, ed. *Today's Poets: American and British Poetry Since the 1930's.* 2nd edition New York: Charles Scribner's Sons, 1972. Besides Patchen poetry, this anthology's introduction discusses Patchen's place in American literature.

WEBB, JON, and LOUISE WEBB, eds. "Homage to Kenneth Patchen," *The Outsider,* 2 (Winter, 1968-1969), unpaged; my pagination 95-138. Patchen's friends and associates remember the man and his influence. Pictorial selections follow him from Greenwich Village to Conn. to San Francisco and Palo Alto. Included in this valuable collection are remembrances by: MIRIAM PATCHEN (94, 138), NORMAN THOMAS (96-97), BROTHER ANTONINUS (97-98), ALLEN GINSBERG (98-99), JAMES BOYER MAY (99-104), HAROLD NORSE (104-105), MILLER BRAND (105-106), HUGH MACDIARMID (107-108), DAVID "TONY" GLOVER (108-111), KENNETH REXROTH (111), JOHN WILLIAM CORRINGTON (112-115), BERN PORTER (115-116), GENE DETRO "Interview, Palo Alto, Calif., Sept., 1967," (116-126), LAWRENCE FERLINGHETTI (128), PETER YATES (128), DAVID MELTZER (129-130), LAFE YOUNG (130-131), JACK CONROY (131-132), FREDERICK ECKMAN (132-133), HENRY MILLER (133-137). Many of these are now more accessible through Richard Morgan's *A Collection of Essays.*

WILDER, AMOS N. "Revolutionary and Proletarian Poetry," *The Spiritual Aspects of the New Poetry.* New York: Harper and Brothers, 1940, pp. 178-195. Early analysis of Patchen as a budding proletarian poet.

WILLIAMS, EMMETT, ed. *An Anthology of Concrete Poetry.* New York: Something Else Press, 1967. Relevant parallel theory of concrete poetry.

WILLIAMS, JONATHAN. Cover notes, *Poemscapes.* Highlands, North Carolina: Jonathan Williams, 1958. An impressionistic analysis of the book.

———. "How Fables Tapped Along Sunken Corridors," in *Aflame and Afun of Walking Faces.* New York: New Directions, 1970, pp. 85-87. Chronicles his transcription of *Fables* in Old Lyme, Conn. Reveals Patchen's automatic methods with interesting biographical details.

WILLIAMS, WILLIAM CARLOS. "A Counsel of Madness," *Fantasy,* 10 (1942), 102-107. Williams's early understanding of Patchen's art, particularly *The Journal of Albion Moonlight,* is sympathetic and insightful.

YATES, PETER. "Poetry and Jazz." *Arts and Architecture,* May 1958. A contemporary's view of the emergence of poetry-and-jazz form.

Index

191